THE EQUITY

MINDSET

IFEOMASINACHI IKE

THE EQUITY MINDSET

DESIGNING HUMAN SPACES THROUGH JOURNEYS, REFLECTIONS, AND PRACTICES

WILEY

Published by John Wiley & Sons, Inc., Hoboken, New Jersey.
Published simultaneously in Canada.

For general information on our other products and services or for technical support, please contact
our Customer Care Department within the United States at (800) 762-2974, outside the United
States at (317) 572-3993 or fax (317) 572-4002.

Wiley also publishes its books in a variety of electronic formats. Some content that appears in print
may not be available in electronic formats. For more information about Wiley products, visit our
web site at www.wiley.com.

Library of Congress Cataloging-in-Publication Data is Available:

ISBN 9781394152193 (Cloth)
ISBN 9781394152209 (ePub)
ISBN 9781394152216 (ePDF)

Cover Design: Wiley
Cover Image: People Icons © Sudowoodo / Getty Images
Author Photo: © Bacilio Bencosme

SKY10052227_072823

To all who march against hate, to essential workers, and to survivors of hostile work environments.

Thank you for showing up and not shutting up.

Contents

My Mommy's Foreword

When my daughter, Ify, asked me, "What work culture do I believe I deserve?," I paused. I may have even repeated it back to her a couple times. Because in my 43 years of working, it is not a question I am used to being asked or even something I am used to thinking about. But the first thing that came to my mind is a place where I would have peace of mind. It's not even about making money, for me. I would have peace of mind. People will appreciate me, and I will appreciate them, and we can still be productive. I would feel comfortable. Because when you feel comfortable, when you are accepted, and you like what you do, no matter how difficult the work is, it makes the work you do easier.

For example, when I started working as a nurse at a rehabilitation center, the fifth floor was the hardest floor to be on. On that floor, there are so many acute issues, including brain injuries. Every move is critical, and everything is urgent. Because of the intensity and stress, nobody wanted to work there. But when I'm asked, "Bernice, can you work double shift? We will put you on the third floor," I say, "No, don't put me on the third floor. It's easier, I know. Put me on the fifth floor." Because even though the work is harder, the people who work there make me feel joy and purpose as I work. We are a team. So when we talk about the culture we deserve, I cannot stress how much environment impacts productivity. And how good people should not be taken for granted. It makes a big difference.

Being an undocumented immigrant when I came to the United States from Nigeria in 1979, with no more than a sixth-grade education, work has always been difficult to endure. The circumstances were not ideal when I landed in New Jersey: I had no green card, and my husband had finished college but without documentation; he couldn't look for a regular job or he would have been deported. And a month after I came here, I found out I was pregnant with Ify. When you don't have certain tools, like education and work experience, the job "option" is the lowest-paid job. And because it's the lowest-paid job and you have commitments and obligations, work makes you put in a lot of hours away from your family. So my first job was cleaning people's homes. I would have loved to be in a position where I made enough money and stayed home with my children, especially when they were little, and watched them grow up. I desire to go back at times to catch what I lost.

And stay a little bit more with them.

Play a little bit more with them.

But the reality is that for the majority of my life, I've had to work at least two jobs at a time to make ends meet. When you start having a family, you want to spend time with them. Our society, however, doesn't value that, at least not for everyone. And that's why when I retire—which is this year—I know I've made it. I will have a new full-time job: being there for my grandchildren, something my children didn't experience. There was no way I could not work. I could never afford to be sick, even though I feel pain throughout my body on a constant basis. But as a mother of five, I thank God, because He was faithful and was there all along, filling the gaps when I couldn't be present. And for that I'm grateful.

When it comes to equity, it pains me, the state we are in. I know there's a saying here: "survival of the fittest." Only the strong survive, I think is the way my kids taught it to me. And in my mind, I wonder,

"Who are we labeling as the strongest? Is it the people with the most? Or the ones surviving the most?" Society has pushed us to spaces where most days, we can't afford to care. Everything is driving us to think it is about "me and mine." Someone could be right next to you at work, dying—even if it's a slow death; their existence is not evidence that they're okay. We have normalized poor people, especially, being neglected. One of Ify's uncles told me about an older rich white man he used to take care of back in the day. They were having a discussion about South Africa at the time, when the Free South Africa movement to end apartheid was happening. Her uncle was so troubled when the response from his patient about the treatment of poor people was, "Forget about the poor, they are used to suffering."

They are used to suffering.

That is a real sentiment driving the apathy and lack of action within our culture. And as a result, so many of us are taken advantage of. We have companies giving big dollars to major causes while treating their own workers without dignity and ignoring their needs, which include comfort and joy. And just because we don't die immediately, it is not lost on me that everything I am was intended to be used up, to exhaust me, to eliminate me. Even when we have to apply for things that may put us more in debt or fill out papers for things we need assistance in, they know people will not read the fine print. And they're capitalizing on that.

They capitalize on the fine print.

And they know many of us can't afford another option.

This is why we need more people with an equity mindset. It is not about having all the answers. It is about being considerate of one another's journeys. To remember how the people you work with got to work, and how their people before them got to work. And why they need to work. Some people go to work hungry: remember that. Some people cannot work because of their disability: how can we fix that? This is not an activity of the privileged or the few. This is about building our muscle to find solutions. And you do not have to help the whole world; some of us are already holding the world on our backs.

But if someone doesn't have a vehicle and they are on their way to work, can you pick them up?

If the only thing separating someone from having a chance is education, can we fill that gap?

If we understand better what people endure, and the history of that burden, then we need to create more solutions. Sincere solutions that actually solve problems, not just use the poor to give the appearance of such. And please don't be two-faced with how you connect with those of us on the margins. You cannot pour out resources with one hand, and then support the systems that bring havoc into our lives with the other. If that's your intention, please leave us alone. It's too expensive to fix up charity wrapped in your public image.

To contribute to this book is a privilege and an opportunity of a lifetime. I am so grateful that I would be counted worthy to pour my insights, and also to be poured into in this way.

Ify, I am proud of you. I am proud of your heart. Ever since childhood, you have considered other people and all others around you. You don't do things because of money, not that you don't deserve to get paid. But I know that that's not what drives you; I have witnessed you do so much for free just because it needed to be done. You have always been that person who just wanted people to be aware and to know what the real story was from under, not from the top. Because when you are under, you see the real truth and the real people. It shows a lot about you and your care for humanity and your concern. I pray that this message will touch people's hands, and they can see that they can help one another from the grassroots. The majority of people who care started from the bottom up. And even if they are not recognized, that labor, care, and concern has resulted in each of us having a much stronger foundation.

Bernice Chijiago Ike
Healthcare professional,
lover of God, Ify's mom

While this book is about equity, I want to acknowledge that my language is not perfect and my practice is evolving. Please know that I continue to build better terminology, awareness, and understanding, and I apologize in advance for any offense or harm I may have unintentionally created. I'm still learning and am committed to doing better.

Introduction:
A Book of
Problems,
Possibilities,
and Practices

Mindsets are powerful. When you hear of a "growth mindset," thoughts of building upon one's skills and continuous learning are likely to emerge. The listener pushes their mind, and subsequently their actions, to align with a more enhanced version of themselves— all because of a belief. One with a "fixed mindset" is assumed to be inflexible and set in their ways, confident in their knowledge of the world and their abilities, and thus not easily persuaded about emerging theories, skill sets, or ideas—especially if what they already know produces a desirable outcome.

An equity mindset has slightly different characteristics from a growth or fixed mindset. For one thing, equity doesn't start with thinking "*What can I improve today?*" An equity mindset begins with questioning one's environment: *"How did this all start, how did we get here, and what does that mean for me and my space?"* Another difference is that while an equity mindset calls for personal journeying, reflection, and awareness, it is not a "self-help" approach. It is intended to support creative solutions-making to address inequities stemming from the consequences of a white-dominant culture. Learning under an equity mindset is not selfish; it's a choice to see one's actions as interconnected, interdependent, and on a continuum with other people and the spaces we exist in. It welcomes those who desire to be accomplices with those who are most proximate to unsafe conditions, generational discrimination, and normalized aggressions. And perhaps most importantly, an equity mindset does not center on the acquiring of knowledge or application of checklists to achieve a business outcome (this is where I may lose some folks, but if you're still here, hear me out).

The practice of an equity mindset is a commitment to:

1. Resisting the practice of normalizing inequity in our spaces;
2. Deepening our understanding of how we got here via data, history, and lived experiences of those with intersectionalities;
3. Leveraging existing tools and frameworks created by those who are oppressed to decenter harmful dominant practices and design through a justice-informed, reparatory lens.

Chapter 1 digs deeper into some of the characteristics of an equity mindset. But to truly understand an equity mindset, we must understand what equity is.

A Working Definition of Equity

The Oxford Dictionary defines equity as "the quality of being fair and impartial." Other versions of this definition include the word "just." An amplified version on Dictionary.com defines equity as "the policy or practice of accounting for the differences in each individual's starting point when pursuing a goal or achievement, and working to remove barriers to equal opportunity." The somewhat problematic part about doing this equity work is that there isn't a solid, shared baseline definition of what equity is. As a result, equity work has largely been watered down, delayed, or minimized to a comfortable, "feel good" or occasional priority. And this matters, especially since at its core, it means that those who need it the most must continue to wait until the masses get it and understand it before they can truly experience dignity, freedom, and safety in every space their bodies occupy.

I'm going to give my working conversation on equity because I think it's important not to assume that everyone has one. When I think of equity, I don't think the definition "the quality of being fair and impartial" is enough. I actually think it can be problematic if one sees the work as being about how to treat others in a "fair and impartial" way without considering the factors which made the current conditions possible. And while I believe that an important quality of equity is an acknowledgment that everyone has a different starting point, that, too, feels incomplete because it doesn't tell you completely convey that not only do people *start* differently but *live* differently. If you only believe that where I started was messed up, you may actually believe that I can do enough work to make up for that start. The mess, though, continues beyond the start, and lasts a lifetime.

My starting point is always this: Equity is needed because inequity exists. Equity is a process to address the gaps in care, support, and resources created by human beings whose intention was to be in power, create systems that benefited from those gaps, and reduce the likelihood that those without power would achieve an equivalent quality of life. That intent has spiraled into multiple mass disparities throughout every system and shows up in virtually every space we exist in. Attempts to eradicate this intent have never fully succeeded, and at times have caused a doubling down of inequitable practices— evidence of how successful the original transplant of divisive beliefs and practices really were, and continue to be.

When equity is described as an outcome (i.e., our goal is to achieve equity through a health-justice lens), it is the state in which no physical, social, or political characteristic of a human being interrupts one's enjoyment, participation, inclusion, or connection to care, support, and resources. By "care, support, and resources," I am usually referring to the first two foundational levels of Maslow's Hierarchy of Needs Pyramid: physiological (water, food, shelter, sex, sleep, clothing, air) and safety (employment, health, property, resources, personal security). Achieving equity would mean that justice (the accountability and repair for harm for the generational impact of inequity, the dismantling of systemically racist systems and practices, and the co-creation of the spaces we exist in) would be present.

The Equity Mindset: Designing Human Spaces Through Journeys, Reflections, and Practices is a guide that refuses to let the opportunity to build better cultures pass us by. Central to this book is that we have enough and we are able to disrupt enough—that is our collective purpose during this time we are here. It's a supplement to the works of those who dedicated much of their lives to telling the ugly truths, like James Baldwin in *No Name in the Streets*; and deepening social frameworks, like what bell hooks in *Feminist Theory: From Margin to Center* did with her call for a deeper intersectionality within the feminist movement; and connecting us to the power of vulnerability, joy, and fighting for our collective happiness, like adrienne maree brown's *Pleasure Activism*. Make no mistake, I don't write as well as these geniuses, but I am connected to the same pulse they and others are, which is the pulse of sharpening how we see each other, how we see our problems, and how we do the most we can with what we got. There are four parts of an equity mindset explored in this book:

1. CENTERING those most impacted by inequity, their histories, and their solutions;
2. CLARITY on how systemic racism is embedded within society, our work, and our interpersonal relationships;

3. CONNECTION to one's personal relationship with power, privilege, and access;

4. COMMITMENT to not just equitable outcomes, but to evolving practices and processes that help us deepen equity, justice, and transformation within our space.

A Creative, Nonlinear, Approach to Delivering This Book

This is not a book you need to read all the way through or in any particular order. I'm hoping that this will be the book you grab when you feel like you need a supporter, a guide, a thought, or an idea. I do not have all the answers. As a person of African descent, I am inclined to bridge truth and practice with storytelling and use narratives, poems, essays, case studies, streams of consciousness, quotes, theories, my ponderings (which I call *ifyisms*), and social commentary as a way to connect and relate truth and honesty—first within myself, then with others. As we are all different learners with different abilities, it was important for me to tap into different methods. This guide is full of diverse frameworks, struggles, and ideas from practitioners and friends who do the work of weaving equity strategies into their space. These #equitymindset insights, chats, and conversations are a way of expanding how we use curiosity as a tool toward systems and culture change. I was inspired by this quote on the power of dialogues, and hope you invest in the richness of the love, the randomness, the ideas that shoot like stars, and the alignment in spirit to create spaces that hold all of our wholeness.

Dialogue is an act of creation.
Dialogue cannot exist in the absence of a profound love for the world and for people.
The naming of the world, which is an act of creation and re-creation,
Is not possible if it is not infused with love ...

No matter where the oppressed are found, the act of love is
commitment to their cause—
The cause of liberation.
And this commitment, because it is loving,
Is dialogical.

      —Paulo Freire, from *The Pedagogy of the Oppressed*

How to Get the Most from This Journey

- **Keep a journal handy!** This book is intended to speak with
  you and support how you connect deeper with your equity
  practice. I am intentional about using accessible language, tone,
  and voices. When a question is posed, or if questions emerge
  for you—write it down!

- **Melt into the dialogues with equity practitioners.** I love
  my tribe; I could listen to them all day. This book is not intended
  to be solely about some of the ways I approach equity. It is also
  intended to connect others with the flow of those who are
  connected to liberation and to identify practical ways for that
  to be real. Whether it's a full conversation or excerpts, dive into
  the very human exchanges about how we view labor, culture,
  and liberation.

- **Connect with Your Team.** I believe in equity moments,
  which are opportunities to pause from the regular pace and
  make intentional moments with your team. As your culture is
  envisioning how to deepen equity, connect on a case study, or
  a dialogue, or a conversation.

- **Supplement What Works (and What Didn't).** This book is
  not intended to be a takeover of existing strategies. It's intended
  to deepen strategy with some concepts that can support more
  sustainable solutions. It's also here to support how you reflect

on past strategies that fell short of reaching their maximum impact. Failing to learn is the true failure.

■ **Do Your Own Personal Work.** Healthy cultures consist of healthy individuals who have done their own personal unpacking. That journey is rewarding, even if at times it reveals scary things about us and our society. If while reading this, you need to pause, do it. And when you come back, reflect on what resonated and why.

■ **If You're Looking For . . .**

Topics	Chapters
Ways to use your leadership within an organization to deepen cultural shifts	14
Space to figure out why Black women bother you	8, 9
Explore why safety is at the heart of equity—and how to create more of it	6, 10
Cheat sheet on consideration when building sustainable pipelines	13
Laws and practices designed to deny persons with disabilities autonomy	7
See what Archie Bunker reveals to us about white supremacism	2
Connect with the equity moments in your personal narrative	11
Unlearn dominant work culture behaviors by asking questions	4, 5
Affirmation that this is hard by design, but you are enough	3

The Lens of the Author: Black, Femme, and Serious about Equity

If Black women were free, it would mean that everyone else would have to be free since our freedom would necessitate the destruction of all the systems of oppression.

—Excerpt from the Combahee River Collective

There are those who may conclude that my passion for equity comes off angry and aggressive. Even though I would characterize my passion differently, I don't fight that definition for two reasons. The first reason is simply that in my life's journey, whether I'm expressing my opinion, in a debate, or I'm simply an observer (and a couple times when I haven't even been in the room), I have been labeled "angry" and "aggressive," which historically serve as dog whistles intended to evoke manufactured tropes about Black women and thus give the green light to those who fear Black women (the underlying emotion of hate) to exert their animus. It's that energy, called *misogynoir*, that adds a unique layer to my work as a problem solver—as do my other intersectionalities—whether they are seen, assumed, or unseen. If your conclusion is that I'm angry and aggressive, my response to you is simply, **why aren't *you?***

The second reason why I don't fight the "angry and aggressive" characterization is because it matches the energy of how inequity was designed in the first place. I used to teach a course that focused on the ways the laws impacted persons of African descent in America. One of the things that frustrated me when I was first preparing to teach the course was how undereducated we are about the fullness of femme labor—both in the Americas and globally. We miss the harsh fact that the starting point of labor injustice for Black women was not that they were prohibited from working. The starting point of labor for Black women was that we were doubly denied: first, our humanity because we were Black; second, any form of protection because we were intentionally denied any protection femininity affords. This is a unique cruelty that is invisibilized, even though what makes us a target is the hypervisibility of our non-European features. My work digs with an urgency to respond to that original sin, and to help others understand why we must do this work, as bell hooks would say, from "the margin to the center."

As the field of equity within work culture and organizations evolves, I unapologetically stand on the premise that if an equity solution does not take into the consideration the experiences, knowledge, and perspectives of Black women and all the diverse intersections under that umbrella, it will not be sustainable. And while dominant culture would have us believe that centering Black lives excludes all others, that is not the reality of the impact of Black activism or policies intended to respond to the unique harms Black people have endured. While my intersections make it likely that I will not be able to escape racism, who I am is an asset to the work that I do and to the many communities outside of my own who have co-labored and benefited as a result of my intersections.

I don't come into this work because it is the right thing to do—although it is. I come into this work with a combined experience of growing up a Black girl in a poor neighborhood, conditioned to believe that education and work would get me out of oppression. It hasn't. I come into this work as a witness to state violence on peaceful protesters. I come into this work as one who continues to use every position I'm in to stretch how power is accessible to those who were intentionally denied it. And I come into this work fighting on behalf of those whose daily lives need people to fight, but their schedules and position in society don't afford them the freedom to fight for themselves. I also am optimistic that equity is bigger than the standard diversity and inclusion (D&I) program, but is a call for dignity in the one activity we all must engage in to even have a shot at a quality of life.

1 | Forty Thoughts on Designing with an Equity Mindset

A mindset is a set of beliefs and attitudes informed by theories, experiences, and one's environment. Failing to inquire why you believe what you believe, behave how you behave, act or fail to act, is evidence of a fixed mindset, which is a threat to how we advance a more humane, just, and equal society.

As mentioned at the top of the Introduction, an equity mindset is about seeing the story behind the unjust social conditions we see today, embracing the opportunity to solve problems, and centering the histories and experiences of multi-marginalized communities. If we're going to build spaces designed for all of us, we cannot just build on top of what we have without accounting for how the systems, practices, and beliefs we currently have are part of the problem. As a result, an equity mindset provides agility and flexibility to the user

seeking to design a new reality. Here is a running stream of characteristics of what an equity mindset is:

Traits and Characteristics

1. An equity mindset is a solutions-based orientation that views
   the identification of the problem and its causes as a necessary
   ingredient toward sustainable change.
2. An equity mindset sees the history of oppressors as a tool for
   reflection, a data source, and a measuring stick by which
   progress should be evaluated.
3. An equity mindset invests in the history of the oppressed as
   evidence of solutions that are centered in love, liberation, and
   inclusion—despite continued marginalization and being
   punished for just being.
4. An equity mindset confronts the relationship between anti-
   Blackness, sexism, misogynoir, ableism, and homophobia.
5. With equity, we must resist picking and choosing data that
   makes us feel comfortable. Practicing with an equity lens
   involves looking at the data, asking "what story is being told,"
   and also inquiring what stories are being hidden.
6. An equity mindset doesn't avoid looking at how sophisticated
   white dominant culture is especially when it comes to water-
   ing down both the harm of systemic racism and the impacts
   of capitalism to Black, Brown, immigrant, and poor communities—or the attempts to prevent sustainable remedies.
7. To do this work is to experience conflict and the many forms
   of resistance to radical change.
8. An equity mindset is laser focused on designing strategies to
   reduce disparities and inequities.
9. An equity mindset is not just anti-racist; it is pro-Black and all
   the intersectionalities Black beings exist in. (And being
   pro-Black does not exclude being pro- anything else.)
10. An equity mindset is agile, adaptable, and aware.

11. An equity mindset is technology that always seeks to disrupt, on purpose, in order to create a new normal: one where we each are seen as deserving of full humanity—not just incremental half-steps toward it.

An Equity Mindset Challenges Us To . . .

12. Accept that inequity is not an accident; it is designed and sustained. Which also means it can be undesigned. But it's going to require a movement.
13. Believe the experiences, knowledge, and expertise of those most impacted and proximate to marginalization.
14. Reconfigure our environments in ways, big and small, where we cannot avoid equity conversations—both the ones related to our work and the ones related to society at large.
15. Commit to ongoing disruption, recognizing that a disruption looks like many beautiful interruptions: a series of mental wellness check-ins, community care, or a protest.
16. Articulate and acknowledge when injustice is happening.
17. Stop blaming oppressed communities for the designs of those in power.
18. Adopt circular ways of learning, engaging in each equity opportunity with the belief that more exposure to equity principles supports better problem-solving strategies.
19. Follow the leadership. Those on the margins. Often. With resources. Without harm.
20. Stop using the limitations of the status quo, including our roles, titles, salaries, reputations as a reason to not act, and instead use those very same assets as tools to bring about change.
21. Abandon what is unhealthy and unlearn how we interact with each other.
22. Believe that each of us is enough to do this work, and that doing the work includes exploring one's own racial identity, history, and journey.

Environments That Foster an Equity Mindset . . .

23. Examine who is in the room, who is not, and explore why the environment is the way it is.
24. Engage lived experiences as data, expertise, and valuable.
25. Consider "What is the most important thing we can do at this moment to reduce the most disparity, increase fairness, and advance justice?"
26. Are open to fight for those who are being attacked, however subtle the injustice may seem.
27. Aren't afraid to say or prioritize "Black." And don't use BIPOC as a way to avoid saying "Black."
28. Block off time to design equity-centered solutions and make such space a part of the norm.
29. Bridge wellness with labor and treat wellness as a priority.
30. Push themselves to be more inclusive than the day before, with acute attention to how those with disabilities are able to maneuver all parts of the organization.

Just and Equitable Work Spaces Feel Like . . .

31. CEOs and key decision makers who are disabled, queer, and femme.
32. Evolved relationships with traditional office culture, even for those whose jobs are connected to a facility.
33. Treating workers as adults, professionals, and contributors— not children or "subordinates."
34. Transformative processes to address harm, with a commitment to ongoing care and constant inspection of power dynamics.
35. Redesigning pipelines and entry points to the workforce and prioritizing dignity, regardless of occupation, salary, or education level.
36. Being worthy of breaks and livable compensation.
37. Free of discrimination, body shaming, or being ignored.

38. Being able to fail and getting the support to succeed.

39. A slower pace.

40. Centering joy whenever possible.

#CultureChat

1. What are some of the characteristics that resonated with you? Why?

2. Which ones feel challenging to you?

3. In your practice, are there other characteristics of an equity mindset that you've observed?

#EquityMindset with Christopher Dennis

Christopher Dennis (he/him) is an equity and inclusion strategist, advisor to senior leadership teams and boards, and founder of the Campus Culture Group.

I think we have been tricked into thinking about our presence and spaces and participation as starting from a deficit mindset off top. So then it has blocked us from being able to compete in the game that is actually being played right now. We over-credentialize, we rationalize, we assimilate in ways because we have to. And we're still effective, to an extent, but we haven't given ourselves the opportunity to know what true health and joy look like, as humans, on a planet. This abandonment, or blindness, or disbelief that we can actually be healthy and joyful while doing this work is subtle, but it's persistent. So when I hear equity mindset, I think there's a part of our identity development that we have to arrive at to really be able to understand

(continued)

how to really tap into our own equity deservedness. Because as we grow and accumulate different experiences, we have to give ourselves permission to change how we leverage our resources.

I always knew social capital played a big role in professionalism, so when you add equity into it, how can you have six weeks of training with everybody, with all the vocabulary in the trainer, and then immediately—every day after training—you violate people by what you talk about?

If we tap into all the aspects of our true selves from an asset perspective, now we can have an equity mindset because I get to bring in everything that I have—I get to wear my locs, we get to have our hair tied up on a Zoom, and we're not discrediting what's coming out of our mouths. There is this thing called "community cultural wealth," and it is one of the theories I'm working with. It takes linguistic capital, family capital, aspirational capital, and others, and I'm using that concept to say, "Be all of who you are, and don't shave off any aspect of yourself to fit into a box." If we're going to have an equity mindset, then the conversation has to change organically, and there are no rules of order that tell me I can't be who I am. For a true equity mindset, one must step into the fear of the unknown, but also have the expectation that you have a right to rewrite all of this, and some days that rewrite may be flipping the table, and some days it might be sitting back and watching things play out. You don't have to be exhausted and die on the vine just because equity is in the conversation.

And I'm also learning that capitalism and people with resources, who have marginalized identities, have a whole different lay of the land. When you have coins in your identity, how do you then not operate as an oppressor as well? Or is it you're actually understanding that you have been under a thumb so long that you want the experience of being the dominant group? It's hard to have, you know, a wealthy person in the room with a person who doesn't have those resources and ensure they're having the same conversation. Both really need to be aware of their own identity development and not judge the other or blame someone—calling someone a victim or saying that someone else has too many resources, especially amongst those belonging to the same community. Because the conversation is the same, they're different struggles.

A couple of thoughts on trauma. People do a lot in conversations and meetings and in policy, based on their trauma. So from an equity mindset, if you haven't acknowledged what this condition has done to you and to people of all walks of life, you are protecting the space that's the safest for you and you think someone is trying to disrupt it or make you process these traumatic things that have happened to you. So wealthy folks, able-bodied folks, hetero, etc., you've still got trauma that you have gone through because of this condition of racism in society. I think about desegregation in *Brown v. Board*—all of the Black and Brown principals, teachers, administrators, who, the lineage of leadership that was designed to really take care of people because it was a mindset of "We're just trying to teach, we're trying to get you right"—we lost that lineage. The cost was great. So from an equity mindset, these incremental changes on things like supplier diversity and other areas—it's like we tried to do a thing (with Brown) to get us all together, and we didn't know that there was a Round 2 that was going to be vicious. So here we are, three years after George Floyd and it's gotten worse. Those funds are drying up in some spaces, and now they want measurables. That's really just another way of trying to protect the bottom line and status quo.

(*continued*)

What we don't have are equity practitioners in power to say, "Can I give folks space to navigate their journey and their agenda, as well as find common-interest convergence for us to get something done?" That's very different than KPIs.

I also realize that with destroying systems—that takes a particular path to commit to that work—versus navigating in systems. Are we going to rebuild a system, or are we going to try to navigate in a system that's imperfect? Two different conversations; you just have to be clear about which one you're on.

When doing this work, you gotta reflect and remember how dope you are and learn to appreciate "you." Revisit your history and revisit favorite memories. Give yourself permission to be and find community—or be by yourself. You won't be able to save everybody, and that's not your job. My job is to be a stop along everybody's path that I come into contact with and say, "Did I honor their presence without limiting my own?"

Be the one where if somebody sees you on their journey years down the road, they're still drawn into what you allowed them to access.

2 | The Work Culture We Inherited (and How It Erases Us All)

I think that the white supremacy culture that all of us have inher-
ited, whether we want it or not, includes this idea that in order for
things to feel right, they have to feel good in our body—that it has
to be non-confrontational to our body. But that's counter to what
marginalized people experience on a daily basis. As a Black person,
my daily survival was designed to ignore my body and instead
prioritize maneuvering external relationships in ways that white
people have never had to think through. If we're going to walk
towards cultures which are just and new, we must accept this fact: we
walk in the world differently.

— Linara Davidson Greenidge (she/her)
philanthropy and equity advisor and
founder of Linara Jinee Consulting, LLC

I can't believe I almost started a sentence with, "kids today have no idea . . ." but the reality is, even though I'm technically a millennial, for us older ones, our television options were far from the vast choices today. It's hard to believe that there was a time when I just watched what was there; regardless of how we felt about the quality of a program, most of us were indoctrinated by the same shows. My parents were pretty strict on what we could watch, but there were a few that either passed their morality test or squeaked by because they didn't get the often lewd jokes. One of the shows they probably should have censored more was *All in the Family* reruns, the seventies hit show that followed the lead antagonist, Archie Bunker, infamously known for his bigoted ideologies. He spared no offense, especially if you were Black, queer, or a woman. But as a kid, he sounded like almost every opinionated working-class white person I had engaged with. I dug around to find some of the episodes that I'm sure I chuckled at as a youngster, but I see the mastery of it today. I tried to transcribe the audience reactions as best I could; there's something about them that enhances the (very uncomfortable) truths this show was highlighting.

Episode #1: Dialogue between Archie and his neighbor, Irene

Irene: The next step is to get them to pay me like a fella.
Archie: What do ya mean by that?
Irene: Oh they're putting me on regular next week, but they're paying me less than the man who used to run the forklift.
Archie: Oh, well, come on, Irene. After all, it's a well-known fact that men are worth more than women.

Crowd laughs with a couple disgruntled "oooohhhs."

Irene: Archie, have you been reading *Playboy*?

Archie: No, Irene. The Bible. And in the Bible it says God made man in his own image. He made women after, from a rib, a cheaper cut.

Crowd explodes with laughter.

Soon after, Archie finds out that Irene is being offered $5.50 an hour—the same as him, which makes him livid.

Archie: Equality is unfair. . .What's the point of a man working hard all his life trying to get someplace, if all he's gonna do is wind up equal.

Question: *How much of this mentality still resonates today? And how does it show up?*

Episode #2: Dialogue between Archie and legend Sammie Davis, Jr.

Archie: If God had meant for us all to be together, he'd a put us together. But look what he done: he put you over in Africa and put the rest of us in all the white countries.

Crowd laughs in disbelief. Sammy's in the thinking man's pose, eyes wide from the ridiculously incredible thing he just heard.

Sammy: Well you must have told him where we were, 'cause someone came and got us.

Audience explodes in a mix of claps and cheers and laughter. Sammy fake-attempts to clean up his response and changes his face to a smiling, non-threatening manner.

Sammy: I mean, there was work for us. How could you resist? Free transportation, room, board, chains . . .

Audience laughs.

Archie: I think you're talkin' about slavery, there, Sammy, and I wanna tell you I was always dead set against slavery.

Audience laughs again.

Question: how many spaces have you heard folks express racist/sexist/ homophobic sentiments, but also try to convince you that they are also an ally?

Episode #3: Family dinner with Archie, his wife, daughter, and future son-in-law, Mike

Mike: I bet you seen a lot of the great ones, huh? (meaning great baseball players)

Archie: Yeah, I seen them all. Ruth, Gehrig, Hubbell, all of 'em. Well before your time of course. Ehh, the game has changed a lot since them days . . . of course, the biggest change of all: 1947.

The audience moans, as if to know what Archie is referring to. Mike is confused.

Mike: 1947?

Archie: Yeah, that was the year they let Jackie Robinson into the Majors. Changed the whole complexion of the game, in more ways than one.

Audience laughs at the double entendre, in both amusement and disbelief at the racism. Mike is visibly annoyed.

Mike: What do you mean by that?

Archie: I mean it threw the whole game outta balance lettin' Robinson in.

Mike: So you think the inferior black race should not be given a chance against the superior white race?

Archie: Hold it, hold it, Mr. Liberal Meathead. I never said nuttin' about your inferior black race, if you'd just let me finish. It's just the opposite if you just let me finish. What I'm sayin' is your coloreds, as is well known, they run faster, they jump higher, they don't bruise so easy. And because of their, whaddya call it, jungle heritage, they see better— it's great for night games.

Very nervous audience laughter.

There's no denying that the genius of the show was the delivery, the punchlines, and the bravery of showcasing white-dominant narratives in everyday life. What Archie illustrates is how myths—like men are better by default, and whiteness is superior—turn into beliefs. We still see many of these sentiments in society today:

- Women are still fighting for equal pay, with Black, Latina, and Indigenous women experiencing the widest wage gaps in comparison to white men;
- Resistance to accurate American history around the enslavement of people of African descent in the colonized Americas is at an all-time high, with attacks in the form of book bans and legislation coming from the highest executive offices throughout the nation;

■ Our medical profession still practices with the belief that Black people have a different tolerance for pain levels, impacting the response to their pain and care they receive.

I don't believe that Archie represents every white person or every interaction between white men and everyone else. Honestly, I don't think that's what Archie's character is intended to do. Archie did not create the ignorance he freely shares; he's a benefactor of a system designed to divide and empower white culture and specifically white men. The show, in a clever way, shows racism and sexism ("ism" meaning belief, system, or philosophy) as a casual occurrence. And while those around Archie are uncomfortable, Archie is not punished for being racist or sexist or homophobic. Instead, he's allowed to lament, as demonstrated through the theme song where he and his wife sing a ballad where the line "those were the days" is repeated throughout. It's very much giving . . . I don't know . . . "make America great again."

■　■　■

Spring is an amazing season, except for one thing: pollen. Pollen covers pretty much everything, whether you can see it or not. It's on your car; it's on your clothes; it gets in your nose. Whether you have a luxury vehicle or you're sneezing during your evening stroll, pollen is in the atmosphere. In many ways, white dominant culture is like pollen. Much of what we experience is informed by what's in the background. And even if we can't see it most of the time, it's all around us, on us and sticks to everything. There's a reason why no matter what profession, Black people are not only marginalized, even the benign solutions—like pipelines and competitions—are soaked with assumptions that the average Black person is inferior, lazy, and doesn't quite cut it. As a result, whereas the majority of average white people do not need to demonstrate above-normal skills or capabilities at every stage of their lives, Black and Brown people must always be at their best.

I hate to break it to some of you, but most diversity pipeline programs aren't dismantling systems. They're perpetuating them. More representation does not automatically result in changes to cultural behavior, or safer conditions for marginalized people to exist in. To do that, a more concerted effort is needed to understand the design of our society—and why every inch of it replicates virtually the same disparities. I created this map to demonstrate how beliefs were embedded within the core pillars of our society, which I like to call the 3Cs: Culture, Cases, and Communications:

WHITE DOMINANT CULTURE
FOUNDATION MAP

I used to teach a college course called *African Americans and the Law*, but it really should have been called *Why America Can't Get Rid of Racism*. The way inequity is baked in is masterful:

- A small number of people in power—white, rich men with property—were not only determining the workforce norms, which included enslaved labor, they were also creating the language to justify their practices. The legal, religious, academic, and medical institutions, all of which were occupied by the same powerful crew, disseminated beliefs about Indigenous, Black, and non-white communities intended to create a unified block to accessing meaningful power.

- While the majority of white people during colonization were too poor to own property, they subscribed to these beliefs and desired to achieve the same status as those in power. This is important, because even today, while there is a clear divide within white communities as to the haves and the have-nots, like Archie, the focus is not on those in power creating the conditions that result in disenfranchisement, but rather on the communities still seeking to recover from laws and narratives that have created a second-class human existence.

- Thus the maintaining of the status quo is not just about those with ultimate power seeking to sustain these divides, but also about an entire culture raised with these embedded ideals—so much so that we fear calling out these practices, and have instead invested in incremental change, even if it means that the majority of Black people, women, queer folks, and persons with disabilities are forced to constantly prove their trauma and humanity just to get the basics.

There are plenty of resources that go into depth about how racism shows up in our society. But what saddens me is that we have demonstrated that data and history don't really matter when it comes to certain lives. And the silence of the majority is why inequity is sustained within our workforce.

■ ■ ■

While Archie presents a comical rendition of racism, it is important to note that this silence also makes working extremely violent. When I think of Archie's fears around change, especially as it pertains to Black people, I think of the scenes of Charlottesville, where white nationalists marched on and around a college campus in Virginia, carrying tiki torches. What feels like something to laugh at for some reminds me of images of hooded Klansman carrying lit torches as they terrorized Black families, which was a recurring nightmare for me when I was a child, so much so that I developed panic attacks that would send me to the hospital. If you were white watching the news about Charlottesville, you may not have felt the same angst that especially Black people felt during that time. I remember being on calls with friends who were trapped in a church that was surrounded that Friday evening by terrorism, hearing how many of them feared that one or more of those supremacists were going to throw their torches toward the church. The sad thing is none of us would have been shocked had that happened.

Perhaps the only thing more shocking than the first night of terror was that we live in a society where hate is so normalized that those demonstrators were able to bring that energy back the next day. And as a result, Heather Heyer, a paralegal who showed up to protest the "Unite the Right" white nationalist protest was killed by a white nationalist who rammed his car into a group of protesters. This type of violence is not limited to demonstrations and protests. The big and subtle ways white nationalist ideologies and the fear of change to white-dominant culture have impacted our collective spaces is connected to the silence of the majority. And it's impacting the one thing almost all of us have to do: work. Here are just a few examples of how this shows up in spaces where people work:

- On October 27, 2018, a perpetrator killed 11 people and wounded 6, including several Holocaust survivors in three Jewish congregations in Pittsburgh, Pennsylvania: Tree of Life, New Light Congregation, and Congregation Dor Hadash. It was the deadliest attack ever on the Jewish community in the United States. Those killed were Joyce Fienberg, 75; Richard Gottfried, 65; Rose Mallinger, 97; Jerry Rabinowitz, 66; Cecil, 59; and David Rosenthal, 54; Bernice, 84 and Sylvan Simon, 86; Daniel Stein, 71; Melvin Wax, 88; Irving Younger, 69. **Synagogues are also places of work.**

- On March 16, 2021, a shooting spree occurred at three spas or massage parlors in the metropolitan area of Atlanta, Georgia. Eight people were killed and one other person was wounded. The victims were Delaina Ashley Yaun, 33; Xiaojie Tan, 49; Daoyou Feng, 44; Paul Andre Michels, 54; Hyun Jung Grant, 51; Suncha Kim, 69; Soon Chung Park, 74; and Yong Ae Yue, 63. **Spas are also places of work.**

- On January 6, 2021, a mob of Donald Trump supporters stormed the U.S. Capitol, seeking to override the will of the people's democratic voting process and determination that Joe Biden would be the president of the United States. The attack resulted in the nation's elected officials, as well as then-Vice President Mike Pence, being trapped in the Capitol—as well as their staffers and workers in the building. Over 130 police officers were injured. At least five deaths were attributed to the incident. **Political buildings are also places of work.**

- On May 14, 2022, a mass shooting occurred in Buffalo, New York, at a Tops Friendly Markets supermarket in the East Side neighborhood. Thirteen people were shot; 10 people were killed, all of whom were Black. One of them was 55-year-old Aaron Salter Jr., a former Buffalo police lieutenant who was working as a security guard when he confronted the shooter. The other victims were Celestine Chaney, 65; Roberta A. Drury, 32; Andre Mackniel, 53; Katherine Massey, 72; Margus D. Morrison, 52; Heyward Patterson, 67; Geraldine Talley, 62; Ruth Whitfield, 86; and Pearl Young, 77. **Grocery stores are also places of work.**

All in the Family confronted truths we're too afraid to embrace today, including how resistance to strategies that aim to destroy the original designs of our culture is violent. The workplace is a microcosm of firmly established beliefs. If we're going to create the spaces we all deserve, we have to explore the painful origin stories of this country, our workforce, and our institutions. Otherwise, we're part of the problem.

#CultureChat

1. What is the origin story of your industry, and how were inequities normalized?

2. Why do you believe so many are afraid to call out Archie's behavior—especially when we know how toxic this is to our collective progress?

3. Which beliefs in the white-dominant culture foundation map show up in your social and professional spaces?

4. Understanding this historical foundation is important because we must know the design before we un-design. What will it take for this to be part of your organizational culture's equity work?

Breaking Bread with History

By Michael Farber (he/him), founder of Breakout

You know, we've grown up very differently. We might have different customs and cultures, but there are some basic drivers. And so while I believe in the power of convenings and gatherings, equity is not about some Kumbaya. Creating space, in a world that doesn't value space to just get to know folks and learn differences, is key. It breaks up something. I think it's important when you can just break bread with someone and hear from someone that you might not otherwise.

I've always been someone who's fascinated by history, and I think there are so many lessons. It blows my mind how late in life I found out about Black Wall Street, and it blows my mind that every time we bring people to Tulsa, they're just learning about it. I was on a call not too long ago and the short story is, the person I was speaking to had to pay for the living survivors (of the Black Wall Street incident) to get to DC, because they were so impoverished that they couldn't even afford a flight to get to DC . . .105 and 107 years old. I think about these things. How even as we, mostly as white society, learn about communities who survive oppression that doesn't necessarily transform their reality, but even from a legal perspective, even if you didn't care about the humanity side, if ever there was a case of property damage and what this community is owed, we should be able to argue that hundreds of millions, if not billions, are owed just on property damage, because that is an American thing. There's a group of people who were massively behind because of damage literally created by the system, approved by our institutions. So, to me, the historical side is important because, being a random white dude in some of these spaces and conversations, I think you have to walk through history and understand the different components that have come into play. Otherwise, if you don't pay attention, you can be like, "I just want meritocracy; the best of the best." In a perfect world, we would want that to be the case, but it feels insane if you don't actually understand the layers and the levels people endure. And why the starting point matters.

I love the concept of ensuring that we're talking about people's aspirations and dreams and wanting what they're building as the center. And it doesn't mean we can't tell historical things that have occurred, but I'm very much like, "We're human, we might be a different skin color, we have different cultural traditions, but we have the same ability to love, and we definitely make things more complicated by maintaining the status quo." So to me, it's really important to constantly recenter. Otherwise it becomes a conversation of "this is what they do and this is what we do" when it should really be focused on the thought that we all want love, want happiness, want families, have hopes and dreams and the ability to achieve when we are respected and given the means and have the necessary backing.

3 | Thoughts on Being an Equity Designer

Whitney McGuire (she/her) is an artist, professor, attorney, and co-founder of Sustainable Brooklyn.

Whitney: I love discussing the power of design because this is what I teach. I'm aware of how, across the board, our systems are designed in a way that is inequitable; that most of the systems we interact with are built with inequitable approaches; and that the root of it all is engineered on white supremacy, and patriarchy, and the propping up of—or the positioning of— people and certain cultures and histories that are considered to be more prominent and more important than other cultures and communities. And so we often have this crisis of omission where design is just not meeting the needs, and it's creating more unmet needs in the process. So as a designer, it's our responsibility, especially as designers from multiple marginalized communities, to engage with the systems that we're trying to redesign in a way that creates agency for

the people or communities that we're designing
for and with.

We also engage by unlearning the fuckery that per-
vades this design world. The facts are that culturally and
historically marginalized communities have been designing solutions because of the inefficiency of the designs
that we interact with on a daily basis. We are forced to
carve out these alternative systems and alternative ways
and use much more brain power just to maneuver
through the world and I think that is a skill set in and of
itself that should be brought to the process of design.

But for designers who may not have that identity of
coming from a marginalized community or having to
really engage with equity as a lifesaver, it is their responsibility to provide frameworks, and resources, and to allow
the communities or people that they're designing for to
have that agency to create the solutions themselves. And,
yes, you have to tap into empathy because no designer is
effective without empathy. You tap into that empathy, but
you do not control the situation. You cannot control the
outcome of the design and even the process of it.

Ify: I love that design inherently has room and runway for
failure. My fear is that the way equity has been seen in
many spaces is that there isn't enough runway to try, test
out, to be curious, to fix, to transform. Empathy is not
just a feeling; it's giving people the space to not only deal
with the mess thrown on them, even the mess they
created, but also providing space to recreate again. What is
further hindering impact and measurable shifts is that
equity has been branded as fun, right? And that's not
what equity is about. Equity is about measuring the
reduction in disparities and bringing forth the necessary

change for humans to be human. So equity definitely has a branding problem. But no matter how much makeup is on it, you're right. It's those of us connected to marginalization who will continue to remind others who dare to design that equity still has to be about meeting the needs and creating the conditions we all thrive for.

And maybe that's what frustrates me about the current muddy PR; the intent of equity-centered design gets lost. So when failure happens, or the perception of failure, or false outcomes aren't met, I feel that there is a double cost to those of us who are practitioners. It forces so many of us to meet these expectations, however flawed, and hope we can hack something in the process. So, now I've got to be entertaining and I've got to present it to you in a way that is accessible, because as much as I don't like it, I also know there are other marginalized persons within that space who deserve disruption. And eventually, I get to a space where true design is possible. But white spaces make you work to get to that point; many aren't confused that it's necessary, but they are hung up on the fact that they benefit from these systemic designs. But even with successful organizational and social designs, I also have to level with you: my gut tells me we haven't given enough time to failure as a part of success in how we design. As you and I know, when one of us "fails," that then means that money gets scrapped, resources get thrown away, consultants don't get called back.

Whitney: Right. I think about this all the time, this failure of definitions and clearly allowing these definitions to inform the ways that we practice within these systems. And equity, in particular, is something that is relatively new. We need time and safety to workshop, and I think

that the urgency really is around the safety to engage
with equity as an experiment with the hope or the
motivation that the tangible outcome will be an equitable
system. But because it has been defined and because there
are so many perceived repercussions for the global minority about getting it wrong—or being perceived as a moral
failure—if they don't hit equity on the mark, within the
six months that they've engaged a consultant or something like that, it's just . . . it's just boggling to me. As if
there isn't 400 plus years of history that we're grappling
with when we're discussing equity, right? We can't even
get to the point where we're discussing the word "equality," you know? So, I completely agree with you and see
why controlling the equity narrative is still centered
within the power and control of white-dominant culture
and desires. And that is doing us a disservice because
equity may always, unfortunately, be seen as a reflection
of them versus a collaborative project that we all have to
support and work towards designing and also become
comfortable with the failures that will come along the
way as we test iterations and feedback loops around
this concept.

Ify: When you're talking it continues to remind me that
equity is about problem solving. And in that problem
solving, we, as practitioners, understand that none of us
holds all the solutions. We accept that if it's collaborative
you come into the space with a part of the equity solution and I come into the space with another piece. And
in the opportunities where creating equity presents itself,
competition is also erased for people who are interested
in problem solving. I think that we are at the tipping
point of what equity design is, or needs to be, especially

for those proximate to inequity within our homes, work spaces, and with our families.

What then does it mean for us to show that there's a different way than the competitive nature of needing to know all the definitions and needing to know all the solutions like that?

Whitney: Yes, we're at a moment where we need to shift how we strategically design solutions with equity in mind. How do we position it as something that is just a natural part of our existence, versus something to get credit for or create an industry in? The same goes with sustainability. Instead of considering it a solution, I'm actually considering looking at it as a problem. That lens better helps me to start strategically designing solutions that can provide more access to sustainability. Similarly, equity, or the lack thereof, is a problem. How do we, then, increase access to it?

As multi-marginalized designers, we can flex in three major ways: understanding the complexity of the problem intimately; taking time to dissect the systems that make up the problem; and finding intervention points we can leverage to design a solution that could possibly turn this whole ship around. But this takes time and I think with the sense of urgency we're currently in, there is this human desire to design without completely understanding the system we have and how it impacts life cycles—the ecosystems we are trying to protect. So, we have a lot of inefficient designs right now and a lot of solutions that fall short. Collaboration, time, patience . . . all these things are kind of antithetical to this idea that we only have X years of habitable planet left. That's why it is so important for designers who have faced crisis for centuries to be positioned in leading both the strategy and the conversations.

We've developed this skill set to deal with legalized oppression and stress at epic proportions impacting our personal lives, our DNA, our lineage—that a lot of the people who are currently leading these conversations or creating solutions just don't have.

Ify: I think often about what would happen if the frameworks that did just what you said already had the resources to flourish. Because in this weird experiment called humanity, there is still an interdependency necessary; equity doesn't just happen. Leaders and cultures make it happen and keep it happening. And in most organizations, that includes having people who focus on just this, on a micro and macro level. Which is why I get concerned when I hear about these mass layoffs of individuals who hold major parts of an organization's understanding regarding equity strategy, whether that's a chief diversity officer, chief equity officer, whatever the case may be. This is a huge problem especially as this disproportionately impacts Black and Brown women, queer folks and those with intersectional realities.

And related tangent: there is also a flaw in how we look at representation; we miss the power in what's possible. You and I belong to the tribe of dark-skinned femme folk. When one of us is in one of those roles, we bring a mindset that is connected to a genius created by struggle and ancestral intelligence. Someone with deeper-hued pigmentation in this world will hold problem-solving insights differently. So again, I'm not looking at just the mass layoffs as a blob, but as an erasure of perspective.

Last related tangent: an acknowledgment that past and current designs are flawed needs to occur. I believe in the power of acknowledgments. Hiring with an equity lens means being creative with how we identify talent. Less linear, transactional hiring. Unapologetically bringing in people, not to meet a numerical goal or check off a box, but, instead, rooted in an understanding that the original design was flawed to begin with. And this person deserves to be here because they inherently are worthy and have value.

Whitney: Yes! So much to unpack here! This whole colonial project is wrong and is a huge design flaw. We have to get to the point where we admit that many of these ingrained and traditional value systems we live with have been wrong, although presented as morally correct. And we must call out that they are creating more unmet needs that are extremely problematic, so much so that we can't even begin to focus on design solutions because we have the wrong foundations to start with. Our whole society is trying to build on a sinking foundation. That's illogical.

It's not impossible to course correct, and I am not hopeless, but we seem to be heading in the wrong direction. Since 2020, diversity, equity and inclusion (DEI) has become more of an industry focus, but a majority of the consultants are still white folks. So what are we doing here? It really shows that we are not ready across the board to accept the fact that people of darker skin tones are marginalized because of what they look like. Because we cannot see this simple, yet impactful, reality is a complete and inherent humanity design flaw by those participating in this system-think. Which means, again, we cannot get anywhere.

So how do we collectively focus on divorcing our experience from this series of failures that have not been our fault and begin to pour more energy and time into solutions that we have been functioning off of for centuries? How do we continue to preserve those and build upon them, and then identify the spaces we can create and organize. Because I don't know if the privileged minority will ever be able to get on board with that, at least not en masse.

Ify: I'm not hopeless either, even though I agree that those in power and with power literally have no incentive to give up such power. That said, I was watching this documentary on Audre Lorde, and, even as she knew she was dying, she made a statement that stuck with me, and I'm paraphrasing, about the importance of fighting the fight even when we know that we won't see the win. I do believe disruptive thought is a win, even though we deserve complete transformation. The fact that we are having this conversation is proof for me that even in our lifetime, we are open to creating works and possibilities that outlive us for others to pick up, put down, critique, and perhaps build with. I think about that immensely when I think of people who were complex enough to go from ideas to overcoming fear enough to write those ideas, preserve those ideas before they transitioned. It's how the design we deserve lives beyond us.

Whitney: Part of the infancy of equity is that we are positioned to really say things have evolved enough that we need to start outlining our theories as to how we have designed around the flaws, and how we will design towards the spaces we deserve. But we also must be bold enough to do this while also divorcing ourselves from the expectation that white-dominant culture will give us permission, accept this as the right way to go, or even recognize it as genius—or as worthy of compensation.

Ivelyse Andino (she/her) is a tech innovator, equity strategist, and the CEO and founder of Radical Health.

When I think of equity mindset, the first thing that it actually brings me to is the first transition, equity into the body. From there I make the immediate jump that equity mindset also needs to be a heartset. I think we spend a lot of time thinking about what equity could be and have these ideals that "if I do this, if I do that, etc." But you don't get there without being in your heart first. The equity mindset requires seeing people as people first, always, at every iteration, whether it is a policy, whether it is a program, whether it is funding. These aren't just numbers, these are people. This is heart, this is mind, this is body. It is a fully embodied experience.

I just did a training which is like the 101 of Health Equity and in designing it, we started with certain questions such as Who are you? What are your values? What are the things that you care about? And the reality is that in order to do this work with integrity and to do it well, you have to know yourself, know your triggers and traumas. These things will always inform what you do and how you do it and for how long. What sustains you? Do you know how your traumas informed you creating trauma in other people? Do you know who you are, in power? And how do you create some of the same systems or be super-intentional every day and make the choice to say, "I am going to stand and be mindful and make space, bring up other leaders, support other people, do whatever it is." These pieces and questions are not easy, but they're necessary.

Many folks are fearful of this work. The two most ancient feelings that we have as human beings, throughout evolution,

(continued)

have stayed with us are fear and shame. As a society, we give grace for fear, but not for shame. We try to avoid feeling shame at all costs, which I think is the segmentation, the stratification, all the affinity because we don't want to feel shame. But the shame is not meant to isolate you. It is literally, maybe an ancient call back to community. It is a matter of accountability, reflection, and a return to "community." This isn't brand new, and it happens over and over again. We make kids do it, right? *Go back and say you're sorry and then go play, right?* And the play might be different, I actually might not play with you anymore, or we may not play in the same way, but we still have to go back to the playground. We still have to go back to the park, and we figure out a new way of being together.

My actual real-life dream for all of this work is a space and a place where we feel connected, where it feels that the edges don't feel as tattered and frayed as they are, but they're actually like mended and blended together.

4 | An Equity Lens: Seeing the Right Problem

If I had an hour to solve a problem I'd spend 55 minutes thinking about the problem and five minutes thinking about solutions.

— Albert Einstein

- How can we get more male teachers of color in the classroom?
- How do we connect more Black families to whole-person healthcare, including quality mental health support?
- Are we able to make rest more accessible to women and femme folk, regardless of where they work?
- Will talented creatives without privileged social networks be able to access careers in industries that pride themselves on exclusivity, including fashion and entertainment?

These are questions I've been asked to solve in my practice as an equity designer and practitioner. Each of these—while speaking to different problems on both a macro and micro level—is connected to the same root causes: they all stem from a white-dominant society with deeply embedded ideologies, beliefs, and practices that dictate who deserves to have a full quality of life. And by "full quality of life," I am referring to a standard baseline of good health, comfort, and joy. In my opinion, access to a full quality of life is the beginning of real human existence and the groundwork of liberation; to be denied access to these basics is to not live in freedom, but in the constant pursuit of what humans should already exist. And when one's day-to-day is preoccupied with achieving the necessary—with no guarantee of actually obtaining it—liberation becomes the dream. To be clear, if one were truly liberated, then one wouldn't dream of having it; one would exist in it, and thus dream of different ways of being, and connecting, and determining. There would likely be no such thing as a "dream job" since labor would not be the basis for obtaining those things we already deserve. People would be dream humans, dream dancers, dream gardeners, dream chess players, dream painters, dream teachers, dream nurses, dream grocers, dream librarians. The preoccupation would be on how to be the best of what one wants to be—not what one needs to be to survive.

As a creative and a dreamer, this vision of liberated persons is what drives how I respond to social problems. As a solutionist, the space of labor is one of many environments where I look to ask the question, "What needs to change for more people to experience more fullness?" As members of a capitalist society, we are sold from childhood on an individualistic notion of input-output; what you put in is what you get. Merit is built on the notion that those who work the hardest get the reward. But I am here as a witness, as are many of you, that this lie has compromised our health, our wellness, and our proximity to liberation. We've all inherited a model that ignores the ways systems were set up to benefit the rich, the white, the able-bodied, and the male. And so the burden of being in a space that honors one's wholeness has been shifted onto those who experience the most harm, the most marginalization. They're the ones who have to figure it out. Until we dismantle this norm, the majority of people will operate in a toxic relationship between our bodies, work, and economics—striving more to achieve more to get more, instead of working in a concerted effort focused on the power structures, systems, and people who benefit from this cycle.

The goal of equity is to achieve the deepest impact possible at any given moment, and to hack as much of the predesigned model to increase the chances that progress will be sustained. So let me go back to the question I posed earlier: *What needs to change for more people to experience more space?* This inquiry is one of the first questions that someone utilizing an equity mindset would ask. Breaking down this question helps build a picture of how equitable strategies should be approached:

- "*What needs to change*" frames the solution as one that requires identifying the root causes of the problem (data) and dismantling what contributes to the problem (disruption) to inform forward motion (design).
- "*For more people to experience more space*" is a demonstration of *flow*: how can our data-disruption-design increase the *flow* of intentionally marginalized communities who are moving toward a different space (destination).

The equity mindset is both a practice and a praxis, both built upon the identification of the root causes of systemic inequities. The mindset theorizes that without an intimate knowledge base of the design of white supremacism (the belief system that white culture is dominant and supreme)—inclusive of its motives and intentions—the sustainability of solutions is inherently compromised. Here's a case study to drive this point home.

Case Study: Where Are All the Black Engineers?

I was asked to come to a tech company with an office in the Washington, DC area. The goal was to support how the organization had created a pipeline strategy to increase the representation of Black engineers. Their first ask of me was to provide a "database of diverse outlets" for their recruitment efforts—I told them I don't do that. When they asked why, I simply said, "I don't know if your space is healthy enough for them." This opened up a conversation about culture setting, and after conducting a culture assessment, I recommended equity mindset coaching across the organization. Using the data-disruption-design-destination structure, this is where we started:

Destination (goal)	Data on root causes and the problems	What we need to Disrupt	Design to address problem
More Black engineers	n/a	n/a	More outreach to diverse databases

Following is one of the exchanges I had during a training session on bias for an all-male group of senior managers:

Me: Why are there so few Black engineers at your company?

Attendee: Many of them may not be good at math. [He missed the point that when I said "Black engineers" I was indicating that they would already be proficient in math.]

Me: So the problem is that we're not good at math?

Attendee: Well, not you. Most people just don't want to do math for this long. Maybe they're just not interested. [Recognizing some of his bias was showing, he overgeneralizes by using the term "people" instead of following through with his assumptions about Black engineers.]

Me: Okay, so let's focus on the ones interested in engineering. Why aren't they here?

Attendee: Maybe they chose a school that wasn't competitive. [This speaks to a potential practice of eliteness and meritocracy as drivers for candidate selection.]

Me: You all are right down the street from Howard. Have you recruited from there?

Attendee: I'm not sure. But we have STEM programs, so folks can improve their math and science. [Again, he reverted to a deficient-based framework, making broad assumptions about why Black people are underrepresented in engineering spaces.]

Me: That's assuming they need support in math and science. Let me ask you this: Are you aware of systemic racism and how it impacts the engineering pipeline?

Attendee: I don't think that's the issue here. We're pretty diverse. I'm here and I was born in another country [he was from Eastern Europe]. I don't think we're racist here.

This exchange is not unique to engineering; it's one I've observed across a variety of industries. While an expressed organizational commitment to diversity existed, the underrepresentation of Black engineers was largely interpreted as a *them* issue versus a larger, systemic issue—including disparities in the K–12 education pipeline. Part of the blame was posed as attributable to Black people: they're just not interested or they lack the necessary merit and qualifications. These notions were largely assumed without any surveys or data points. And while there were a few Black engineers, none of them were in management. This means that potential candidates would not see someone who looked like them in leadership within the organization. Other than a desire to be in more "diverse" spaces, there was no strong sentiment around disrupting any existing practices or strategies. Finally, evidence of anti-blackness within the management team was initially downplayed as "natural bias," something that they believed did not impact their decision-making processes or culture.

So what do you do when a mostly homogeneous organization with a mostly white male leadership team is looking to increase representation?

This is a question many organizations confront. And like many organizations before, their previous engagements with specialists had focused on broad diversity and inclusion goals, recruitment recommendations, and management training on bias and inclusive practices. One of their senior HR directors expressed frustration about the gap between that investment and the attrition data, including low promotions for women, virtually no presence of Black and Latina women engineers, and Black engineers exiting before their third year. I requested a leadership meeting with senior leaders and managers. Based on both her understandable frustrations and some of the feedback from the senior managers, I wanted to ensure that those who had the most authority were clear about the ways they needed to show up for their strategies to flourish.

Better Understanding of the Problem

While equity was not a major part of their prior work, the leadership felt they were automatically doing equity work because they hired a DEI specialist. I wanted to demonstrate to the leaders that an equity mindset enhances existing diversity and inclusion strategies, but depending on the practitioner, equity may not have been fully explored. As a foundation, I reviewed with the team commonly referenced words to ensure we were working from a shared understanding of definitions:

- Diversity is the presence of difference within a given setting. Seeing individuals as "diverse" is not correct. There is no such thing as a "diverse candidate." Diversity is a measurement of the differences that exist within a collective or a group. So a team can be diverse, but a person cannot. **It is possible to have a diverse team that does not represent individuals from**

multi-marginalized communities. Diversity, alone, also does not guarantee safety or the erasure of racial aggressions and other psychologically unsafe behavior. Diversity is an OUTCOME.

- Inclusion is about folks with different identities feeling valued, being valued, leveraged, and welcomed within a given setting. **Organizations with more diversity among their managers and strong accountability standards for how their managers find ways to value everyone on their team have better chances of success than organizations with minimal standards of accountability.** Inclusion is an OUTCOME.

- Equity, as an approach, is a PROCESS that focuses on the art of achieving access to opportunities and using data to learn how to address barriers and create better systems. Equity recognizes that advantages exist disproportionately, and as a result we don't all start from the same place. Equity is a process that begins with that truth, acknowledges that unequal starting places impact choices and journeys and works at correcting and addressing the imbalance—meeting needs where necessary for human beings to thrive. **This is the dominant definition used in this book.**

- Equity, at times, is also described as an OUTCOME (we are aiming to achieve health equity). In this manner, practitioners are looking to achieve a state where communities are not denied access based on their race, gender, sexual orientation, ability, or poverty.

- Intersectionality is a framework to describe the phenomenon of how people of multiple marginalized identities are adversely treated due to the unique biases that stem from the combination of those identities. **Intersectionality is not just about "traits" or "differences" or even multiple identities. Intersectionality is about the experiences of people burdened with the overlap and compounded oppression that comes from the normalized discrimination toward each of the identities they hold.**

I make no apologies for my stance that outcomes-driven work solely focused on the outcomes of diversity and inclusion does not automatically mean equity is a part of the work. That said, when diversity, inclusion, and equity are working with each other, they provide different dimensions to problem solving and build off of each other. Here is a demonstration of typical questions for each:

Diversity Questions	Inclusion Questions	Equity Questions
How can we get more "diverse" people into our pipeline? How can we incentivize recruiting "diverse candidates"? Why aren't people of differing identities applying for our jobs?	What is the experience for individuals who are underrepresented within the organization? What barriers prevent people with marginalized identities from feeling a sense of welcome and belonging? What don't we realize we are doing that is negatively impacting our new, more diverse, teams?	(If we value diversity) How are we responding to trends concerning underrepresented talent within our company? (If we believe in representation) What is the composition of our leadership structure, and why does that matter? When we look at gender parity, are we accounting for those with intersectional realities? What is our accountability system for continuous improvement?

I then asked senior leaders what assurances do Black engineers have that their full selves, including their journeys leading up to the organization, will be honored, respected, and not minimized? I followed up by asking a series of questions around mentors, sponsors, and support programs. And I inquired about the path to management should a candidate be interested in leadership one day. It was starting to dawn on them that the issue wasn't Black candidates; the issue was a lack of internal accountability measures focused on equity.

A culture assessment of the organization revealed some really insightful aspects that had been normalized. There were biases against historically Black colleges or universities (HBCU) candidates and non-Ivy candidates, individuals labeled as "diverse hires," and immigrant employees. These emerged as top themes. The invisibility of women and their contributions was also a leading theme. And failure to understand privilege was identified as a barrier to inclusion within the organization. The "good ol' boys" syndrome was also a factor. I also flagged lack of responses to concerns with senior managers, little to no transparency around pay and promotion processes, and lack of safe reporting mechanisms for grievances. They were seeing more clearly that their organization was benefiting white men and that without interventions, they were not going to be able to sustain a diverse culture.

To be clear, these are issues that occur in many other industries. I pointed out that because they did not have a clear picture of their internal problems, their original solution—diversifying their outlets to recruit more Black engineers—was not only the wrong one, it would also have resulted in the same outcomes they were experiencing with attrition. So we needed to set clear intentions about the path forward.

Setting Intentions: Vision, Commitments, and Tracking Equity Outcomes

The culture had raised its concerns and offered solutions. The ball was now in senior leadership's lap to design a road map. They wanted a six- to nine-month plan, which would give them time to try things out while also moving toward real milestones. I wanted them to reflect on the mindset needed for the current and future team, including what it means to be a manager of teams with diverse backgrounds and specifically Black people. I also wanted them to reflect on what they need to commit to learning and evaluating as a form of continuous accountability. They were asked to create a vision statement with priority foci. Then they were asked to create two lanes of action: an outcomes track and a learning track. They had four major assignments, which I encourage organizations to answer for themselves:

Assignment #1: What is the new organizational equity vision? In other words, what is the organization committed to, what does the organization stand for, and what is its specific stance as it relates to addressing the root causes of inequity and social injustice?

Assignment #2: What are the specific priorities the organization will focus on to further this mission?

Assignment #3: What are the outcomes for each of the major culture stages that align with the vision and the priorities? And what are the major strategies to achieve those outcomes?

- Recruitment
- Leadership development and diversity
- Career paths and professional development
- Inclusion and safety

Assignment #4: Finally, what are the learnings and experiments the organization uses to test out how to create a more sustained impact?

Out of this effort, some of the real gains included:

- Ambitious goal setting: they had a recruitment goal of increasing hiring of Black, Indigenous, and Latino engineers by 25 percent within a 12-month time frame;
- During that same time frame, they committed to increasing the diversity of senior leadership by 25 percent with specific attention to people of color and women;
- Investing in anonymous reporting tools to increase safety;
- Creation of an internship program for rising engineers;
- Equity included as part of the management evaluation;
- Yearlong investment in understanding root causes, their impact in the field of engineering, and connecting with diverse thought leaders on their experiences.

Embedding a Statement of Acknowledgment

When shifts are happening, it is important to acknowledge where power and privilege exist. An understanding of the power dynamics promotes truth-setting and an opportunity for cultures to heal in ways that aren't frequently practiced within cultures. I love using the framework from the Anti-Oppression Network as a model because it weaves history with the realities of today and invites everyone to be a participant in shaping the culture through an equity mindset. Here is their framework:[1]

Safer Space Policy/Community Agreements

How we work together.

Everyone, regardless of social status has equal opportunity of participation, and all members of the steering committee/board and general membership need to ensure that in all processes of working together equal opportunity happens.

Inequality exists everywhere (whether we like it or not), even in social justice spaces. Gender identity, gender expression, sexual orientation, dis/abilities, ethnicity/ethnic heritage, race, age, size, class, and citizenship status are some of the more obvious examples of how people can be marginalized.

We also live in a capitalist society that measures our worth by outputs and outcomes, and quantifies our production and productivity. This is an ableist model, which we want to move away from by setting our own agenda and do things because we want to and need to, not because we feel pressured to.

Members agree to lessen the negative effects of as many of these oppressive ideologies as possible, because they are all interconnected and relevant to our work. This is done through commitment of learning and unlearning through workshops, policy-making, community collaborations, etc. and can be done collectively.

Members have the right to a safer space where they feel their contributions have worth and are comfortable to share their needs, assert their boundaries, and develop their agency.

Members shall seek meaningful and inclusive mediation to help resolve conflicts within the group. All parties involved must agree with the process. This should be done with a third party outside the group that has no conflict of interest (unless no options are available, a third party with experience with conflict resolution reflective of our group constitution and guidelines is highly recommended).

Group members are accountable to each other and the community at large, and are responsible for direct and open communication, transparency, and how we share and distribute power.

How we create, implement, and ensure safer spaces.

Group guidelines/community agreements/safer space policies will be created by and for group members sharing any given space, i.e., steering committee/board, subcommittees, community gatherings/events.

Group guidelines/community agreements will be reviewed at the beginning of meetings each time a new person has joined.

Group guidelines/community agreements can be elaborated on with stories for clarity and understanding.

Group guidelines/community agreements are working documents in continuous development, and will be reviewed and up for modification every other meeting.

What started off as a request for a list of diverse outlets evolved into internal intention-setting using data, collaboration, and centering the truths about how bias manifests within organizations. An equity mindset is not a magic pill. It simply tries to understand the problems before it and asks, "What's the best we can do with what we got?" (a phrase inspired by Mariah Carey).

Beyond "Diversity Hires" and Toward Sustainability

By Agu Onuma (he/him), Attorney

Equity supposedly began when I accepted an offer in the tech space. That's a big deal to companies: the offer. But because we don't have the same tools to negotiate and advocate, we, as Black people, kind of get left behind. When you get into the job it's very important to have a diverse group of employees in order to feel that inclusivity. When you are the only Black person on your team, you feel set apart; I often did not feel included. It was not an equitable space.

So how can I be successful with all these variables working against me and I don't feel that I can connect with others I work with? It's almost a recipe for disaster and failure when the people you work with cannot engage and relate.

Over the last decade, I think the initial goal was "diverse hiring"; now the goal should be about sustainability. Companies have figured out the hiring part, but what are they doing when it comes to pipeline, to growth, to success, to recognizing the differences in employees and making sure that employees have the resources in place?

For example, in the tech space, growth and success have to do with sponsorship. In corporate America, without a sponsor you almost always fail because there's no one at the table to advocate for you personally. And that really is the bottom line. So a company needs to recognize that employees need both mentorship and sponsorship, which are two different things.

A mentor can pour into me the soft skills that I need, and they can point out what it means to be a Black man and how I should act in professional settings, how to communicate, and they can give me the same tutelage and training whether they are an attorney or not. But a sponsor is someone who has power, who has access to the C-suite, the decision-makers—whose approval will mean a lot to help define what your trajectory and career are.

You're not human in corporate America, you're just a number. You think you have value until the company decides one day to let you go. And so again this is the importance of having the sponsors and proper mentorship and proper work life balance, because at any day all of this could come crashing down and no one's gonna call you and ask, "Are you okay? Or say, "Here's some money, take care of yourself."

5 | Testing Assumptions About What Our Cultures Must Be

One of the first times I recall using the term "equity mindset," I was serving in senior leadership within the New York City mayor's office, focused on advancing programs for youth of color throughout the city. While the word "equity" was thrown around here and there, I was confused about what lens the administration was utilizing to identify the problems it sought to solve. I wasn't even sure we were on the same page about whether equity was a problem-solving process, or just code for "diversity." My experience as a public servant has been that many government programs that centered on communities of color, with an expressed mission to address disparities, were actually exacerbating inequities and reinforcing harmful beliefs about marginalized communities.

So many well-intentioned programs are greenlit without deeper scrutiny into its design. One such program was called the Fatherhood Academy—an offering that involved 14 governmental initiatives providing various services to help *"fathers become more active in the lives of their children."* After engaging with community leaders and fellow municipal employees, I recognized there were narratives about father-hood, particularly Black and Latino fathers, driving how the coalition moved and ultimately designed programs. Probably the strongest assumption was that men of color weren't involved in their children's lives and programs were needed to motivate them to reconnect. The usage of data was also quite problematic, as statistics on Black and Latino dropout rates, connection to the legal system, and unemploy-ment rates were often presented more as stereotypical tropes rather than being presented as evidence of larger, deeper social problems.

During one of our leadership roundtables, the topic of discussion was low attendance of Black and Latino men in the offered programs. After listening to each leader tout how much they had invested in these efforts, and their confusion as to why men weren't just "drop-ping into" their doors, especially since everything was free, I said to myself, *Oh shit, these folks are about to blame these Black and Brown men for their failed programs.* Cultures that start with disappointment toward the audiences they desire to engage seldom create authentic and sus-tainable remedies. At that moment, I introduced a different line of questioning to test some of the assumptions in the room, in the hopes of opening up the conversation and recentering our priorities:

- Why are we focused on Black and Latino men, solely? What evidence do we have that supports the notion that they are less connected to their children than their counterparts?
- If such disconnection exists, what are the contributing factors? Are our services acknowledging the impact of societal inequi-ties, not just from a data standpoint but also from a human-centered approach? In other words, have we created space to ask our desired audience what their life experiences have been to put a narrative to the stats?
- Do we have a sense as to how the compounded realities of poverty, poor education, and racialized profiling have impacted one's emo-tional and mental well-being?

- How are we messaging these programs to our desired audience? Is "Fatherhood Academy" as a name empowering for adults? Are we approaching them from a place of blame and judgment? Are there ways we can glean from them what welcoming, humane, and engaging language and environments would feel like?

My voice, I'm sure, shook the entire time; as the only woman in the room, while I had the title, in no way did I ever act like I had the power. But to my surprise, a real conversation especially with those who had a personal connection to the ways systems create hardships. The responses to these questions were so vibrant, rich, and creative. It was recognized that more insights were needed to answer the questions, and so mixed methods of fact gathering were executed—from focus groups and interviews with Black and Latino men on their experiences. One of the rewarding parts for me was sharing with the roundtable many studies that debunked the myth that Black men were more absent from their children's lives than their counterparts. In fact, data revealed the opposite: Black men are the most involved with their children, regardless of which parent had custody. We even got down to the root causes of how these prominent assumptions and stereotypes about Black men became mainstream, stemming all the way back to slave codes, which morphed into Black codes and Jim Crow and progressed into policies like COINTELPRO and the labeling of the economic and health crisis of the 1970s and 1980s as a "war on drugs."

The experience opened up more questions than answers and invited us to not only reclaim truths about the ways racist beliefs show up in government programming, but to push back and ask key questions about the approach of our work, and government programming, as a whole:

- Who are we deeming as "experts" in social policy and public service work?
- If we all don't have a shared equity mindset and test our assumptions, methods, and processes, then what is guiding what we're doing?

- Are we truly advancing the most strategic efforts and programs? Or are we participating in the cementing of systemic negligence and oppression?

■ ■ ■

White-dominant culture is the status quo. Virtually all of our institutions exhibit the same dominant behaviors and cultural norms. What is important to understand about white-dominant culture is that it impacts every aspect of our lives, including:

- How we're socialized;
- Our expectations and definitions of success;
- How we view justice and injustice;
- How we build culture;
- Our proximity to power, privilege, and access.

Because of its widespread normalization, white-dominant culture is often unquestioned, unchallenged, and unnegotiated. Institutions and work culture were historically built upon four main tenets: (1) white supremacism (the belief system that white culture and standards are superior to all other races and ethnicities); (2) anti-blackness (the actions, practices, and behaviors that minimize, marginalize, or devalue the full participation of Black people in life); (3) misogyny (the ingrained prejudice, dislike, disregard for, and hatred toward women); and (4) exploitative labor. As a result, our work culture is saturated with problematic behaviors that have remained relatively constant.

I want you to think about your organization while looking at this list and identify how many of these characteristics show up within your workspace:

- Staff feeling that they are not invited to, or have limited freedom to, offer different ideas in problem solving, decision making, and major culture or work decisions.

- Failures are attributed to individual mistakes without any assessment of the organization's systemic impact.
- Lack of transparency and accountability in decision making.
- Colleagues and peers experience "iced out" moments for speaking up about culture issues, advocating on behalf of colleagues, or calling out leadership or problematic parties.
- Individuals within the organization holding back perspectives and insights so as not to cause conflict.
- Internal communication processes that set up distinct groups of haves and have-nots for access to information.
- Discussions about outcomes in which numbers trump other forms of data.
- No clear understanding of how one can advance vertically, or no rhyme or reason for how one becomes a manager or supervisor.
- Ineffective follow-up to issues of racial aggressions (which includes microaggressions), sexual harassment, or hostile work environments.
- No system in place to evaluate the organization's leadership.

These are just some of the common activities of organizations with leaders who refuse to address white-dominant culture. And because these characteristics go unquestioned in a society that centers the individual rather than systems, those already farthest from power—particularly disabled persons, queer people of color, and women of color—are also faced with invisibilized harms. Compound that with the fact that the majority of higher-paid roles exist within cultures that are majority white, underrepresented communities are overexposed to aggressions without safe outlets to address them, even as their social mobility increases.

This is in part why representation is important, especially for those with intersectional realities. Having a critical mass of diverse experiences within a work culture—with acute attention to how those belonging to multi-marginalized communities access positions of power and decision making—is a powerful equity design feature that advances safety and aids in supporting how cultures identify and respond to white-dominant norms.

■ ■ ■

Creating a culture with an equity mindset means not taking the status quo wholesale. It also is necessary to be aware that even when things seem fine, white-dominant culture is still present. We don't need to wait for harm to happen before confronting the white-dominant culture; we assume it exists and ask how it shows up in our workplace. The power of testing assumptions is that it simply asks questions: *Why do we do things like this? And must we keep doing it this way?* Its goal is not to point fingers; the goal is to confront the especially toxic parts of white-dominant culture and to use curiosity and questioning to redesign better behaviors for the culture.

Here are some questions that help cultures identify common practices which may actually be contributing to more harm:

DOMINANT CULTURE PRACTICES vs. TESTING ASSUMPTIONS	Traditional Practices	Testing Assumptions
	Patriarchal leadership style	How are we defining leadership that works for us?
	Unaddressed sexism	What trends should we be observing to assess gender equity?
	Frequent racial aggressions	What are our responses to race inequity?
	Desire for linear, quick solutions	What would continuous support look like?
	Merit-based awards	How do we celebrate and reward each other?
	Invisible Intersectionality Analysis	Do we even know what those with multiple oppressed identities are experiencing?

As you go through these questions, preferably with your teams, ask yourself the following:

■ What are the problem areas revealed during this process?

- Where are there differences in perspective?
- Are there topics some members are uncomfortable discussing?

While the responses to these questions may feel uncomfortable, and even embarrassing, don't stay in that space. Don't just rush to action either; lack of a clear vision, strategy, and commitment to learning and accountability threatens the sustainability of the organization's impact. In the words of author and activist adrienne maree brown, "What we pay attention to grows." If we're going to build spaces for our current and future selves to work with dignity, we have to hack our environment and adopt different learning behaviors and systems to track progress.

Establishing New Learning Behaviors

Testing our assumptions is a practice that helps us develop new cultural learning behaviors and different methods to achieve equitable outcomes. Every stage of our work life cycle is impacted by dominant norms, and as such ought to be interrogated. Because we absorb cultural norms through formal and informal channels, creating new ways of being requires identifying a desired outcome and adjusting our performance and progress behaviors. Performance behaviors are implemented actions that are intended to increase equity. Progress behaviors are actions that are laser-focused on how to measure improvements and meaningful shifts to conditions. This is important because it normalizes a rigor around course correction and ensures that equity efforts move beyond simple intentions. Performance behaviors and progress behaviors are overlapping concepts, which together consist of the ongoing activities the culture commits to in furtherance of a goal—and the measurements used to determine if we are, indeed, moving toward our goal. If it were an equation, it would look something like this:

Equitable goals = weaving equity mindset (performance behaviors + progress behaviors)

Here are some examples of what this could look like:

Example 1: Culture A determines they want to increase the number of community college graduates after their culture assessment revealed that they had virtually no one from that population (equitable goal). Culture A determined that each recruiter would engage with 10 campuses across the country and hold a job fair per semester (performance behavior). Managers have been advised to check resume submission rates for the next 90 days for any spikes in interest (progress behavior).

Example 2: After testing assumptions about managerial promotions, Culture V discovered that most managers—all men—were recommended by other senior leaders—who were also all men. Recommenders claimed they went through the internal manager recommendation program; other team members who'd expressed interest in being considered to be a manager claimed they had never heard of this program. Furthermore, reports of hostile work environments, micromanagement, and favoritism made many question whether the current managers should remain in their roles. As part of their organizational culture intervention, Culture V committed to a more transparent communications strategy for when promotional roles opened up, implemented a manager's apprenticeship training course, and connected aspirants with senior sponsors (performance behavior). They also committed to race and gender parity within their management team over the next 12 months (equitable goal). A consultant was retained to assess the manager's leadership performance (performance behavior) and recommended that all managers be trained in anti-oppression work, organizational management, and emotional intelligence over the course of the next year and that those with repetitive incidents of unhealthy behavior should be considered for termination (progress behavior).

As both examples demonstrate, goals, progress, and performance are interdependent. They require big, medium, and small actions and commitments. They require tracking for accountability. And they use time frames as a way to be intentional and to adjust strategies if needed.

#CultureChat

Explore each major stage of your organization's work life cycle and answer the testing assumption questions with your team—and see what other questions emerge. Then identify new behaviors, and some equitable goals, performance goals, and progress goals.

Work Life Cycle Stages	Testing Assumption Questions
Recruitment and hiring	How are we hiring and based on what? Is the data telling us anything about our biases?
Onboarding and new hire expectations	Are we providing any guidance on the expectations of our culture as it relates to equity?
Culture maintenance	Is there a standard of "professionalism" that is expected? What does it look like? What does it sound like?
Attrition and retention	What trends are emerging with regard to who stays and who leaves? Are we measuring work satisfaction? Do we know why people are leaving or deciding to stay?
Recognitions and promotions	How are employees rewarded, and what trends, if any, emerge? What is the composition of our managerial staff? Who is not in management?

(Continued)

Work Life Cycle Stages	Testing Assumption Questions
Leadership	What is the composition of leadership? What has their involvement been with the deepening equity within the culture? How long has each member been in leadership? How are we describing diversity? What marginalized communities are not represented within senior leadership? Why?

The Struggle to Get Beyond the "Buzz" of Equity (and Commit to It)

By Alexis Confer (she/her), Political Strategist and Movement Builder

The last five or six years have been a huge change for me in the way I manage and govern, and even understand, equity. As a white woman, I recognize that I have to be mindful of how I carry myself in different spaces, the type of teams I want to be on, the teams I want to build, and the type of bosses I seek out. But I think in the last couple years, when there's been such an important focus on how we're doing advocacy, particularly around such a traumatic time like COVID, everyone's so interested in getting back to "normal" that we're losing some of the moments and pressure points that the last couple years identified for us.

I first tasted the fruits of equitable practices when we worked at City Hall. Our team was diverse, and it was the first time I sat back and recognized and felt, with not just lip service, what it means to have space for diverse ideas, diverse backgrounds, diverse bodies—all of that. It was the first time where I saw the role I could play as a white woman, side by side, for system change. In that process, I also learned more about what implicit bias was and how it existed and the way it played out in meeting after meeting. I recognized that there were actual tangible skills I could use as a hiring manager to change systematic problems.

In the last couple of years in the advocacy space I've seen people really struggle to change best practices, but in my recent projects working with Gen Z, they're not always sure how to implement some of these changes yet, but they do have a lot of good ideas for the world they envision and we all deserve. In listening to them and others, I found myself overwhelmed and thinking that there is so much to change all at once, which I think is the mentality of so many people in this space. That kind of feeling of, "How will we do all of this?" is overwhelming plenty of advocacy spaces. I'm fortunate to have had a head start because of the people I've had around me all the years; people who I've seen model it.

I'm worried that people don't know where to turn and also don't know the difference between the buzzwords of the moment. You see this with mental health, for example. I find it hard to believe that most internet influencers who are speaking about mental health have clinical backgrounds to help people deal with mental health. I'm glad that we're talking about it, that thrills me, but I feel there's a similar thing occurring with equity. People don't really know the definition of equity, but are trying

(*Continued*)

to speak on it. So that's my worry that when people get back to business as usual and are worried about their bottom line, I just don't want equity to be a fad.

I can't speak for all white people, but the truth of my equity journey is that I've always wanted to be good and do good in this world, and perhaps my faith background has something to do with that. I don't, however, think I really understood the concept of equity. For those who have never delved into this space or are just hearing the word "equity," how do we catch them up without overwhelming or fear of fatigue and burnout? People don't want to take on this tough work. And that leads to the other thing that worries me: the correcting for optics in a way that's almost tokenizing and doesn't actually value equity. I can't tell you how many times I've been reached out to by recruiters who request diverse candidates, and I'm thinking, first off, an individual can't be diverse, a group of people can be diverse. That mindset is problematic on many levels. I mean, do you want that selected person to be the face so they can talk about how your organization is so great? Is that person going to get set up for success once they're in there? Are they actually going to have the support they will need as a Black woman running an organization or whatever it might be? These are some of the things I now worry about since being exposed to equity and what it means.

It took me years to receive the feedback about what and how my whiteness presents in these spaces, and I have learned to be open to having real, sometimes uncomfortable, conversations about the part white people play. Unfortunately, people are so afraid to talk freely, afraid to say the wrong thing, particularly white people, and the result is that we can't even reach the point of discussing solutions together.

#EquityMindset with Rebecca Cokley

Rebecca Cokley is a notable philanthropist, activist, and equity pixie.

Ify: Rebecca, talk to us about your equity journey.

Rebecca: Ify, I think about our friendship origin story. I share it all the time I think about sitting in that room at the US Conference on Women and me being at this long table and you and Jesse being on one side and me being on the total opposite side. And we'd never met before. The panel started on your side, and the icebreaker was about what we were all there to do; what was the point of all this. And you and Jesse both bring up ableism. Even to this day, I have never been in a space where someone else has brought up ableism before I did. It made me want to cry. It allowed me to be seen without speaking, which as a disabled person I don't often experience and was a game changer.

I share another story about one of my friends, Brittany, who saw via social media that a whole bunch of us were at the National Conference on Independent Living. It's like the biggest disability conference. And it's the last day of the conference, and we were sitting in the lobby, and she said, "You know, I think I consider myself disabled. Because I live with depression. But at the same time, I sit here in a space, and we're sitting in the lobby, and there's a line of people all waiting as a wheelchair user is trying to get in the elevator. It's hard to feel that their experience and my experience are parallel."

And I said to her, "Okay, let's unpack this a bit. Does your depression impact how you eat?"

She pauses and then was like, "Yeah and I've been eating crap all this week. It's like the second week in a row."

"All right. Does it impact what you wear?"

"Girl, this is my first time not in sweats."

"Okay, check. Does it impact how you engage with your loved ones?" She showed me all the ignored calls from her family for the last several days. So I was like, "Welcome, we've been waiting for you, our community is infinitely strengthened by your presence. And we are better for you being here."

She kind of laughed. "No one's ever said that."

And I told her that I honestly believe that it's radical to welcome people into movement spaces. I told her that what she's dealing with is no different than what they're dealing with. Does their disability impact how they eat? Yeah. The power of the definition of disability is that it says, "Does your impairment impact your activities of daily living?" And of course, that'll vary depending on the person. Both stories really come down to how we hold each other in these moments.

Ify: And in some ways it's getting harder to hold each other. As we're talking about creating spaces we all deserve, how do we make sense of it all when it feels like many of the gains we've made are being erased?

Rebecca: It makes sense to think, *Does this even matter?* I actually go back to a conversation I had with Congressman John Lewis and sitting in his office right after Trump got elected and literally flopping on his couch and being

like, "Alright, JL, what do we do?" And we joked a
bit—we have long history; my grandfather threw him in
jail. Like they were archnemeses. So I was like, "What
did we do in this moment? You are the only person I
can think of who's still around for me to ask how we
move forward." And he started pointing at the pictures
on the wall. And each friend had a different complicated
story. Friends who suffered physical and psychological
disabilities due to Vietnam. A couple who at one time
were in an abusive relationship, but no one did anything
because they came from a family of Black doctors and
funded the movement. Another one was addicted to
crack. But Congressman Lewis told me that he called
him just to talk. And he said the most important thing
we have to do in this time is to hold on to each other.
And to not let us be separated, and to address those
things across our spaces, within our movements that
need to be addressed. Not letting the silent go unsaid.
He said, "They're gonna try to divide all of us because
they know that we're all coming together. The old heads,
the Black Lives Matter folks, the DACA kids, the sun-
shine kids, like all of these groups, are finding ways to
come together. And that's terrifying. But that's the
power. The biggest thing that y'all can do differently is
to like to hold each other. Hold on tight." And I remember thinking that his advice was a good place to start.

Ify: Movement building is so much work and so difficult. We
all benefit from movements, but it truly is the labor of
the marginalized and the oppressed. If I can be honest,
for people who come from intersectional realities, to
have both the burden of being under-recognized for

how they maintain culture, in their workspaces, in their organizations—literally being geniuses, innovating our way through oppression—and also the burden of enrolling people and convincing the masses that this is the direction we should go. All while surviving. What are ways we can reverse this dynamic?

Rebecca: I work in philanthropy. And there's a real challenge getting folks inside of philanthropy to operate with an intersectional lens and operationalize it. Not saying "gender over here," "race over there," "disability over here," and whatever the next thing is. But actually saying "how do you train? Can you train a mindset? And if you can't train it, then what do you do to help people understand in structuring grant dollars? Can you ensure that it is weaved throughout the DNA of the grant? And like, what can you do contractually? And how do you ensure that you are advocating for those whose labor is the reason why the organization is getting the funding?" I'm seeing this happen specifically with Black staff and all the intersections: Black and gay staff, Black and disabled staff, but also they're not the CEO, so the CEO is getting the credit, but you're funding the work of this one person, or this one division or whatever. Then as soon as the organization gets the money, they either get terminated, or they get gaslit out of the organization. I pulled a grant a month ago from a major white LGBT organization because the person whose work I was funding is Black and queer. And literally as soon as the grant application was in, they started gaslighting him out. And he called me, and I was like, "Oh, well, then we're just not funding this." I literally wrote the organization and said thank you for your submission. We received numerous applications. And it is clear to us that we are not on the same page And so we won't be moving forward. And did I send it to them on the Friday of a long weekend? Sure did. Purposely, so I could ruin their entire weekend? Yes, I did.

For me, it was simple: I would not have thought about funding this organization, if not for X person working there. I mean, I know the organization—their work is highly regarded in all of the things. But the person is someone who has always come to the table with a really unique analysis to the work that they were doing; there was no one else in the organization that could do it. For me, it's about the reward side: how can I use the privileges that I have, whether it be building the money, the connections, whatever it is, to actually shift the makeup of the leadership of these organizations, and I know that starts with money. I know if I invest, if I make grants to support the research being done by Black women and top-tier universities, they are more likely to get tenure. And that's a big deal. And so, you know, when I first came that was like, they made grants to three disabled Black women at three different universities, because they're doing amazing work. And are the white folks doing that work? Yeah. But is them being at the university going to shift anything? No. But if I give money to a Black disabled woman professor at Stanford, who's looking at the ADEA and prison and Black women and girls, that shit matters. If I find Brittany Wilson at New York Law School is building a civil rights and disability justice legal clinic, that shit matters. Because every student and group of students that come in that door are going to learn from that professor; her writing is going to get moved; their writing is going to have such a bigger reach, because they're now a tenured professor at X University, and they've also gotten a Ford grant. And so in those instances the investment in the individual is as important, if not more important, than the investment in the work.

6

Are Your People S.A.F.E.?

At the core of an equity mindset is how we maximize safety for those denied access to it. Almost all organizations desire safety for their team members, but until safety is achieved, it is just an intention. By recognizing that lack of safety has a ripple effect on other aspects of security, increasing safety increases the chances one will not only be satisfied while working, but one may successfully move from just trying to survive to actually thriving within their organization and beyond. The creation of safety practices fills the gap between the desire of an organization and the actual experience of a safe environment. A safe environment is not an environment absent of harm, but one that is intentional about acknowledging it, addressing it, and being flexible to explore alternatives when existing solutions are no longer serving the culture. Safety, like equity, is thus more of a process, not a set of static tools and offerings. And it starts with an assessment of key considerations:

Are the people in your culture **S.A.F.E.**?

Seen holistically

Access to support

Free to be in, and address, conflict

Encouraged and radically affirmed

Seen Holistically

Let me share a real scenario between a former consultant and I who was underperforming. Let's call her "Kelsey":

Me: Hey Kelsey, so I see that there's been improvement since the last time we checked in. My files feel way more organized and accessible—thank you. I'm still having some issues with the scheduling. I'm not getting the supportive documents I need in time enough for the meeting. Sometimes the zoom invite is wrong. And a couple times the other party wasn't invited. Not sure what's up but wanted to hear a bit about where the breakdown is.

Kelsey coughs and adjusts her glasses and computer.

Kelsey: I'm so sorry, I'm really trying to be more mindful. I didn't even know there were that many mistakes. I guess they're just piling up (rubs forehead) and you have a lot of work, and I don't want to hold up any momentum and I'm trying to be as responsive as possible and I . . .

Kelsey coughs again.

Me: Okay, pause, we'll get back to that. What is going on with *you*? In this moment, how are you feeling?

Kelsey proceeds to share that she was not feeling well and possibly had COVID. She also shared that her eyes had been bothering her and may be impacting her at work. After I asked about the tiled walls in the background, she shared that she was in her bathroom and staying away from her grandmother as much as she could to minimize the risk of spreading anything. We talked a bit about the pressures she was experiencing, some of her prior experiences with other managers, and the "fear of failing." When we shifted back to the work conversation, we set different expectations for that week to prioritize both my "must haves" for the week, but also the healing time she needed to tend to her body.

As a visually impaired person, it's important for me to stress that when I say one ought to be "seen holistically," I am leaning into the alternative definitions beyond sight. To see a person holistically is to position yourself in a space of examining what another person needs to function cooperatively. Studies show that work can be an isolating space, often being a microcosm of "us/them" dynamics, a drive to be perfect, and closing off the personal things in our lives, which are equally, if not more important than our work. Grind culture, however, perpetuates a (very false) "leave your problems at the door" attitude, leaving those within the culture, and disproportionately women of color, queer folks, and persons with disabilities (and acknowledging that a person can be all three, as well as other intersectionalities) enduring the feeling of being invisible, socially isolated, or misunderstood in silence. Not only is this soul crushing, but it's actually counterproductive to the overall goal of doing great work. The art of discernment is not about assumptions, but awareness. Pausing to notice where one has made progress, one's genius, and that someone is not 100 percent is not only gracious, it is human.

I don't want it to be missed that in the example I gave between Kelsey and me, it did not matter that she was an extension of our team as a consultant—she was still a part of the culture. And even though the conversation started as being about certain expectations not being met, that did not erase the opportunity to be observant, or "lessen" my ability to be direct about my needs. Asking more about where Kelsey was "in the moment" provided valuable insights that helped both of us find solutions that helped us both win. Creating space to more than the surface of our peers and team members is an act of mutuality; one day, you, too, will need to be seen holistically.

It is worth adding that the point is not to be a therapist. It is to simply be just as invested in the person as you are in what they can produce—and to also honor when they are producing, showing up, and doing well. This works laterally, vertically, and diagonally—positionality or power doesn't stop us from practicing seeing others holistically.

Some examples that may help you *see holistically* include:

What you're sensing or inviting in the space	"Seeing holistically" examples
• Signs someone may be unwell, tired, or frustrated • Want to give a person a breath • Great way to begin a conversation	*How are you feeling in this very moment? (I like using in vs. at because it invites one to breathe inwardly and take a note of themselves outside of work.)*
• Signs someone may be feeling rushed, pressed • Want the person to know you value their time • Great way to use time as a way of seeing them, without hinting that anything is "wrong"	*You know what, we have an hour, let's talk for about 45 minutes and I'll give us back 15—does that work?*
• Appreciation for another's contributions	*I know this isn't the point of the conversation, but your remarks in the last full-team meeting really got me thinking differently. Thank you!*
• Recognition of an issue still in process	*Just want you to know that I did receive your concern about the tone of some of our peers. I'm working on how to address it and am actively seeking support and suggestions.*

The key here is to lean into increasing awareness, not assumptions. Slowing down to get to know those within your community is an act of resistance. It's important to respect that each person within our space is mid-journey, personally and professionally; we each deserve to be seen regularly.

Access to Support

There are four major forms of support that I look for when assessing the health of a culture:

1. **Harassment and discrimination support:** Ensuring team members are aware of policies and reporting standards, and also being specific about the consequences for those who contribute toward a hostile work environment, including patterns of racialized, gendered, and homophobic aggressions. Support for those who experience such incidents should also be clear and articulated, including ways to report anonymously and emotional and mental health support, if needed.

2. **Environmental support:** Attention to the actual space where their team members work, including how responsive they are to requests for hybrid and remote work, alternatives to the five-day work week, quality equipment for diverse environments (i.e., a laptop and headset for remote options), and how disabled team members are experiencing the entire accommodations' process—from request to utilization to troubleshooting. Even for roles that require one to physically be connected to a building or facility, imagining how the space can support one's care and off-work needs is part of how we design deservedness within built environments.

3. **Professional support:** Setting up team members to succeed in their roles and clear articulations of what "success" means to the organization, and what a team member should be

doing if they are considering vertical senior roles—or desiring to explore other opportunities within and outside of the organization. As the term "professional" has largely been framed to mean how well individuals fit within the status quo, professional support needs to broaden to include how managers and leaders are trained to address their biases, observe trends in promotions and advancement opportunities, and create intentional pipelines for underrepresented communities to advance into leadership.

4. **Mental health and wellness support:** Resources team members can tap into to address their socio-emotional well-being, ranging from mental health days, directories of resources and articles, to access to therapists, healers, social workers, and life coaches. Also recognize that therapy is not the answer for everyone; be open to the variety of ways your culture speaks to wellness needs and destressors.

The current white-dominant work culture narrative includes not trusting those within our spaces to make decisions about their mind, body, and space. This patriarchal way of being creates hurdles to support, applies rigid rules as to how people can access such support, and often requires justification or evidence to be validated by the powers that be. Compounded with bias, one of the byproducts of this phenomenon is that women of color, particularly, are the least likely to request days off and tend to accrue more sick days and vacation time than their counterparts. Much of this is attributed to fears about financial security, perceptions of Black and Brown people being "lazy," and the belief that being seen physically working will increase the chances of advancement and promotions. The pressure is even more intense for those who are not physically able to be in traditional work spaces and are thus limited in how they demonstrate not only their work, but their leadership abilities.

It takes time to create a culture of support that tackles accessibility, historical oppression, and overall well-being. An equity mindset takes all of this into account and designs opportunities to encourage rest, amplify the leadership of disabled team members, and deepen their understanding of why diversity in leadership is vital to the wellness of everyone within the culture—and those to come.

Deepening your culture's support is an ongoing journey. When assessing if your culture is **S.A.F.E.**, here are some starting steps regarding access to support:

- **Declare Humans Deserve Support. Period.:** Support must be a part of the success recipe for a just culture. Create a culture declaration stating the importance of support and the organization's commitment to expanding support, encouraging support, and being accountable for the access to support. Centering that every person is worthy of support is important.
- **Create a Support Map:** A support map shows all the existing supports within the organization—as well as how the community is made aware of the supports. A landscape analysis can help you kick off this process:
  - **Do we have policies for the following, and if so, how do members get access to it? In other words, where does all this live?**

Harassment and Discrimination Support
- Sexual harassment policy that provides examples of what qualifies as sexual aggression, hostility, and assault
- Racial discrimination policy that addresses misogynoir, racial aggressions, and discrimination on the basis of skin color, hair, and name
- Disability discrimination policy that outlines the culture's stance on ableist behavior, examples of how it shows up, and mitigating practices

- A confidential and/or anonymous process to report harassment, discrimination, or other hostilities
- Anti-oppression training for all team members, including those in leadership and management
- Experts, mediators, and counselors

Environmental Support

- An accommodations process, listing the supports we currently provide, how to request those supports, and how to request supports not immediately available
- A flex work policy that includes remote and hybrid options
- A care and support policy for those who have to be on-site, in the office, or whose performance requires being in the same space with clients, customers, and/or patients

Professional Support

- Formal and/or informal managerial and leadership training process
- Sponsorship, mentorship, and/or apprenticeship programs
- Access to diverse career coaches and technical support trainers
- Encouragement when failures happen

Mental Health and Wellness Support

- Mental health days
- Caregiver support policy
- Parental leave policy
- Mental health first aid training for all team members
- Directory of culturally responsive wellness first responders, including therapists, healers, and social workers
- Free, stipend, or financial support for professional mental health services

- **If the answer is "no" to any of the above, what are the culture's thoughts around the policies we do not currently have? Are they needed? What does an implementation strategy look like?**
- **Connect with the Culture:** Whether you're a century-old organization or a startup, communicating existing support infrastructure with the culture and getting their insights and feedback is part of infusing equity in processes that traditionally only involve senior leadership. Keep track of how information is shared with members, as well as the frequency with which such information is shared. Be open to support recommendations and provide timely responses whenever a team member is offering alternatives and diverse solutions.

Free to Be in, and Address, Conflict

There are few things more tiring in the workplace than trying to make white spaces feel comfortable with me. As a Black woman with a darker complexion and Afrocentric features, including full lips and strong cheekbones, all my life I have been told that I'm intimidating before I speak. I am assumed to be aggressive by my mere presence. When a legitimate issue would arise, my former self would have to muster up the strength to walk into spaces and, at times, act completely counter to their imaginations of me, just to get to a temporary resolution. For several of my non-Black women colleagues of color, they have expressed similar rituals, whether they were perceived as "timid," and thus got backlash for being outspoken, or they were gaslit and told the issue just wasn't that big a deal, killing any real dialogue. And for many of my queer friends and siblings, awareness of how "big" their expressions are before audiences with traditional "professional" standards occupies so much time and energy.

While there's much talk about psychological safety, achieving that space is difficult because of all the ways we've been socialized to not only protect white voices and agree with them, but to dismiss other communities of color, and to be especially hostile and aggressive with Black people. And to be very honest, maneuvering conflict is difficult if you haven't done your own personal racial healing and equity commitment to evolving and learning. White-dominant culture is often framed as conflict averse, and that is true to an extent. But from law firms to leading nonprofits, I have seen tempers, emotional outbursts, and tantrums flare, and they are mostly by white people. And here's the thing—I actually don't have a problem with that. My issue is everyone is not able to access that liberty. Conflict—and the space to express emotion freely without fear of repercussion—is, thus, a privileged activity often reserved for those with the most power. This also means that in most spaces, tropes and stereotypes about marginalized groups will drive how conflict is perceived and handled. The default then becomes toxic positivity, with its cousins passive-aggressiveness and avoidance being the main vehicles by which conflict is managed (or not) within a space.

An equity mindset means having a different relationship with conflict. Here are some strategies that organizations can leverage:

1. Acknowledge the many ways white-dominant culture creates barriers and hurdles for non-white, non-straight, and disabled team members, and set the expectation that each person will engage in racial healing journeys as a means of maintaining a healthy environment. This includes engaging those in power if the organization embodies a hierarchical structure.

2. Continually express that conflict is inevitable and that it provides an opportunity to improve systems and gain better understanding of another team member. That said, people should be encouraged to create boundaries and share what those are with the community.

3. Identify culturally diverse and connected coaches, mediators, and third-party culture facilitators who can be called on for one-on-one, two-party (or however many are directly impacted), or full-team mediations. Having a person all parties trust is key to resolution.

4. Normalize conflict-resolution strategies as part of professional development and what it means to be a member of this culture. An example of this could be team active listening practices, alternative dispute-resolution training, or required readings or listening tools (a book club vibe or a podcast focused on conflict).

Quick digression: a client of mine required that the entire team, from staff to consultants, read a book called *Crucial Conversations*.[1] Every week for about 20 minutes, we would dissect key themes and relate them to experiences we were encountering as a team. For a second, I was like, "I don't know about this." Until one day a colleague requested a "crucial conversation" with me. Because of my own personal anxiety with conflict, my immediate reaction was nervousness. But what gave me ease was that based on her signaling, I knew how to enter the conversation—and also how she would initiate the dialogue. Whatever the tool is, a shared understanding about the resolution process supports how parties enter in a conflict—and also exit.

5. Explore with your culture how a transformative justice framework may support sustainable community building.

What is transformative justice? A transformative justice framework looks not only to resolve the conflict at hand, but also looks at an environment as a whole to address how the culture evolves from harm. Here are some ways a transformative justice process differs from a traditional grievance process:

Traditional Grievance Process	Transformative Justice Process
• Fact-finding	• Addressing underlying harm
• Process looks backward	• Accountability plus reconciliation
• Focus on the person who caused the harm	• Collective vs. individualistic
• A consequence is created for that person and thus the conclusion of the process	• Responsive to both interpersonal and structural harms
	• There is a goal of building, keeping, and repairing relationships, AND community

Transformative practices embed tools to support how communications, safety, and support are normalized within a culture. This is extremely powerful because it flattens the power structure and engages the full community to develop agreements, commitments, values, and practices before conflict arises. Accountability is very important, but unlike traditional grievance processes, punishment is not the goal. Before, during, and in between conflicts, the community prioritizes practices to promote the following:

■ Healing and repair
■ De-escalation strategies
■ Analyzing power and alternatives to white-dominant culture settings
■ Harm reduction, safety, and respecting boundaries
■ Collective responsibility of the culture
■ Social transformation

The beauty of this model is it holds all those committed to addressing their healing while tending the culture at large. Through the support of facilitators and third-party culture guides, the team as a whole engages in a journey of mitigating through an equity lens and relying on the culture to support when harm arises. Skills learned from this process are transferable to other spaces, transporting this equity mindset practice into another culture that undoubtedly would benefit from its implementation.

Encouraged and Radically Affirmed

Just as it is great to be seen, it is also great to be affirmed and encouraged. A culture that is safe supports the journey of each of its members, and that includes how one wants to grow and how one wants to lead. One of the leading contributing factors to women leaving the workforce is lack of affirmation, as well as invisibility and low morale support for leadership opportunities. And let me put it in context: in a society where Black women make 65 cents to every dollar a white man makes, Latinas make 60 cents, and Indigenous women make 51 cents to every dollar, the lack of acknowledgment of labor only compounds this economic injustice. A promotion for a woman of color is an opportunity to bridge that gap a little more and become more socially mobile. Affirming women doesn't look like paying attention to us every March. In the words of Beyoncé, "Pay me in equity."

I remember training a travel-industry leader in London. During the training, I asked everyone to introduce themselves and asked them to share their pronouns. One of the guys said, "Oh we all know each other," and everyone, including me, laughed a bit as he punched the shoulder of his co-worker (it was a love tap, nothing violent). I simply replied, "Well, I don't know, so how about you go after me." So I did a simple modeling, sharing what I was comfortable with, and he went after me, and the next person, and so on. One of their colleagues said their name and responded that their pronoun was "they/them." Everyone sat in that for a minute, until the same outspoken guy said, "But we know you like girls, it's okay." His colleague replied, "It has nothing to do with that, and I'm happy to talk with any of you about it.

But I like they/them. And I'm so glad I was asked to introduce myself." It has been almost a decade since that incident, and I've evolved in my introductions, including encouraging folks to introduce themselves however they'd like—with or without pronouns. But what was evident from their body language and engagement for the remainder of the training was that the opportunity to be affirmed in their fullness freed them up to engage with their colleagues more authentically and richly. I also learned from them the power of inviting people into your space. Regularly engaging the full culture in conversations about how they want to be celebrated, acknowledged, called, and seen invites a different relationship between a human and the space they work in. As the African revolutionary leader Amílcar Cabral described culture as the "collective personality of a people," we have to be invested in how each person is safe just "being," and how they are not hindered from personal and professional growth opportunities.

#CultureChat

- What are the ways you'd like to be radically affirmed in your work space?
- What would encouragement within your space feel like? Who would you like it to come from?
- Are you encouraged to lead and grow within your organization? If so, what are the conditions that affirm you? If not, what do you envision would need to shift for that to happen?
- If invited to share some of these thoughts with the full culture, would you? Why or why not?

Creating a Support Plan When on a Budget

As a founder of a Black femme-led boutique consultancy firm, mental wellness was a priority from the time of formation. That said, resources are a real consideration. The strength about being a smaller team is that I get to have more one-on-one interactions with each of my members and am able to see them holistically and explore different options with them. I learned early on that each member desired a different outlet. For some, it was traditional therapy, while for others it looked like dance classes or a cannabis retreat. Providing a wellness stipend (disbursed quarterly or bi-annually) fostered flexibility and removed me from their individual determinations of health. Coaching support, team mediation, partnering with local healers and health practitioners for discounted rates, and being creative while traveling for work are other ways wellness has been prioritized. I've also created a budget for unexpected life realities, such as team members needing to get home for an emergency or loss. Being transparent with the team has also helped; communicating what we can offer, how people can request as-needed support, and what we hope to offer in the future is received positively and sets healthy expectations for everyone within the community.

Companies need to take racial discrimination issues as serious as issues related to sexual harassment and assault. And really, both need to be taken way more seriously, and industries need to be prepared for a constant flow of concerns. Because both happen so frequently because of the culture we've inherited. I understand that it might be somewhat difficult to measure at times,

(Continued)

but companies need to start taking it seriously and calling it out. When someone is sexually assaulted on the job, the company jumps to action. It needs to be the same with racial issues.

—**Tyshaia Earnest (she/her), fashion consultant and Creative and Culture Strategist at Pink Cornrows**

Who Holds the Responsibility for Safety and Care?

By Nana Gyami, (she/her), Attorney and Executive Director of Black Alliance for Just Immigration

We want more caring models, right? Okay. But even if we were to have models of care, who holds that labor?

When it comes to immigrants, particularly Black and Brown, it is frightening to know that the majority of our discussion about their importance is connected to their labor, not their humanity. And it's no surprise that they are disproportionately in the care industry—an industry that America has systematically undersupported, with the exception of doctors. So much of equity, however, is about care and safety. When we talk about "creating just cultures," we are emphasizing the value of those energies that have been considered non-masculine. But as we do that, who is being asked to carry that weight? *We're going to be more empathetic, we're going to be more compassionate, we're going to be more caring, we're going to have more conversations, but who is being asked to lead those conversations? Who's being asked to head those well-ness task forces?* We are once again being told to be the mule, right? Who do we associate with that type of work? So I think there are a couple of pieces to unpack here. One is, what's been normalized? What is made to seem like it's the model you want to copy? And then when we're undoing that and trying to untie those knots, who are the people sitting up here pulling with their fingernails to get these knots untied and being tasked with holding the energy to keep that going?

A crucial part of this work is self-acknowledgment; that is necessary and also hard to do. We need to understand and redefine what our expectation is for ourselves and determine where we got the expectation from to begin with. If you've been told your whole life that what gives you value is being the best at blah, blah, blah and now you sit down and say, "Well actually, that's not critically important," you're actually having to say that something you value that you have been taught and colonized into valuing, you have to let that go. And this is why merit—participating in meritocracy—is super difficult to break. Once you start to do that, you feel a sense of freedom that makes the shackles hurt because you initially thought they were bracelets—but now they need to come off. Then you can move to "what does it mean when we finally are decolonized? What does it mean to have an organization that is decolonized of these notions of work?"

7 | Remote Work Is a Reasonable Accommodation (and We Owe the Disability Justice Community an Apology)

Discussions about mental health cannot be seen as a luxury, which is why I will continue to advocate that remote work is one of the most equitable things you can do.

— Amber Cabral, inclusion strategist and founder/ CEO of Cabral Co.

There are so many angles we can enter into the conversation about why remote work needs to be a part of as many organizations as possible—including how it not being an option could pose serious issues with retention.[1] What we do know is that we have proved in a relatively short amount of time that we can do almost all professions outside of a physical building; we are able to balance work and life, even during stressful moments like the pandemic; and mental health and overall wellness can be incorporated into our schedules, and is now something job seekers look for when pursuing their next endeavor.

Many leaders embraced remote work, as they were able to see that there was relatively little to no threat to productivity (which in a capitalist society makes sense; if the sausage is making money, who cares how it's made). Yet and still, there is an ongoing struggle of "to be in the office, or not to be in the office, that is the question" that I've come to recognize more as a fear of management evolving and an attachment to white-dominant norms of "seeing" people working to believe that it's real. There are a lot of equity aspects we can focus on to drive home why remote work made sense during the pandemic and how it created a window move forward with a different vision.

But I also want to hold space for disability justice advocates who were calling for remote work to be a reasonable accommodation before the pandemic, if only for the reason that almost every human will, at some point in their lives, have a disability. Simultaneously true, human beings in a capitalist society have to work. And finally, with what we know about COVID-19, those with certain disabilities are more susceptible to infection and face greater hardships and risks to their lives. Some of these challenges also compromise the uptake of life-saving vaccines and medications, resulting in virtually zero virus-fighting antibodies to fight off certain infections. An equitable response would, thus, acknowledge that remote work should be employed as a risk-mitigation strategy—both from contracting and from spreading.

Under the Americans with Disabilities Act (ADA), an employer must provide a reasonable accommodation to an employee with a disability so long as the employee's accommodation allows a person to perform "essential job functions" and does not cause an "undue hardship" to the employer, which means "significant difficulty or expense."[2] You may or may not have noticed, but the reason why the majority of workers were able to take advantage of mass remote work is because most of our responsibilities were deemed "essential job functions." Those functions, which are typically listed in job descriptions, thus signal to an employee that this role can be performed outside of the workplace, and that such accommodation will not be seen as above and beyond the ability of the organization. This is important to note because disability advocates have been saying this very same thing for such a long time. **So why haven't we been listening to disabled people up until now?** It's worth identifying some of the origins of ableism in this country—and why it should have never taken a pandemic for a significant part of our population to be able to work, and to work with dignity.

Have You Heard of the "Ugly Laws"?

I have to give credit to disability justice advocate Dara Baldwin, who presented during one of our Black Policy Lab conferences on the topic "Building a Disability Curriculum." In this session, she asked participants, "Have you heard of the 'ugly laws'?" Even as an attorney with a background in civil and human rights, I had never heard about them. When I did, it blew me away. Here is an example of an ugly law, this one from an 1867 law in San Francisco:

> It is illegal for *"any person, who is diseased, maimed, mutilated or deformed in any way, so as to be an unsightly or disgusting object, to expose himself or herself to public view."*

Here is another one from the 1881 Chicago City Code, demonstrating the cost of being seen with a disability:

Any person who is diseased, maimed, mutilated, or in any way deformed, so as to be an unsightly or disgusting object, or an improper person to be allowed in or on the streets, highways, thoroughfares, or public places in the city, shall not therein or thereon expose himself or herself to public view, under the penalty of a fine of $1 for each offense.

It is worth noting that $1 in 1881 is more than $20 in 2023. As those with disabilities were considered undesirable, and the presence of their disability was deemed an unlawful "exposure," employment for disabled persons was always a challenge—and still is to this day. Persons with disabilities endured the double burden of the stigma of their stigma and the punishment for having a disability, often resulting in isolation for fear of being seen in public, or being in debt due to fines, or even imprisonment.

Ugly laws—with origins of eugenics beliefs stemming from sixteenth-century England—existed in the books until 1974. For context, that was six years before I was born. No matter what laws came after 1974, the sentiments, attitudes, and perceptions toward people with disabilities is baked into our standards of professionalism and has contributed to the economic marginalization of millions of people. The additional identities of race and gender compound this oppression, increasing the lack of safety from racial and sexual discrimination, harassment, and assault.

Even when folks have a job, there are still significant stigmas within work-culture norms that impede the progress of those with disabilities. This is really important to digest, not just in the context of work accommodations, but also in the overall psyche of our society. Even if we have remote work options, that is not where the equity work ends.

Humanizing This Topic

Meet Natalia Díaz, Public Policy Professional

Ify, I know you call me an expert, but you're the only one. I'm seen as an expert of nothing. I mean, if I have to be cheeky, I guess you could call me an expert of my life. But I can't even say that because people question me about my life experiences all the time. I could say, "The sky is blue," and immediately someone would say, "Hmm, I'm not sure." Last time I checked, I had cerebral palsy, not colorblindness. But nope, I could never be right about my life. I'm constantly questioned about everything.

Whether in my personal life or in the workplace, I'm not believed. You probably don't want to put this in your book, but I hate online dating. There's this notion that I must be catfishing someone because my disability is not visible. But when I get on the phone, I'm asked, "Oh, did you have a drink?" And I say, "No, I have a speech impediment." Then a slow fade, exit stage left.

In the workplace, I also see similar strains of questioning what I say because of how my words come out. I am literally saying the same thing others are saying. I'm bilingual, so I speak English and Spanish very well. That said, I am always at the mercy of who is in the room and often only validated when people who have higher titles acknowledge me.

Some of the things we need to confront in the workplace and all spaces is the misconception that disability automatically means a mental capacity issue or learning disability. And I'm sure that's not the right language; I'm also a product of society and use ableist language all the time—and I know that, right? So there's this weird thing that you hold as one with a disability—doing the labor of distinguishing yourself from others with disabilities, especially as it relates to mental or learning capacity,

(Continued)

while also knowing that humans who do have different disabilities than mine also deserve wholeness, solutions, and supports to ensure they can work and live, too. So if you're not doing the equity work of disability justice, we're not equipping people with the proper language.

When discussing an equity mindset, realize that focusing on the workplace is way too late for a person, a woman, a woman of color like me. The first thing that is stripped from persons with lifelong disabilities is choice. As a child with a disability, you were taught that you don't own your body. And I have found as a young adult, and even still now, very difficult to unlearn because people are touching you against your will all the fucking time when you're a child, in the name of medicine. But let me break down what you are conditioning a child like me to accept from as young as three months old. When your physical therapist touches you, it hurts. Same with when the speech therapist is literally holding your face and forcing motions with your mouth; you don't have a choice in those settings. Because that is their job, at least that is what you are taught. You are conditioned to allow someone else to tell you what is best for your body. And that is very difficult to unlearn.

So knowing this, advocacy for us is not a one-time ergonomic chair or an advocacy toolkit. It's complex and requires training people in new behaviors. I was lucky: I had parents who intervened as a child when I was a baby, but there were still obstacles. I never learned to say no, to say, "I don't want to do that dumb shit." And to all those who want people to come back to the office—I have so much to say about this, but I'll leave it here: many of you just told on yourself. You didn't care about any of us prior to the pandemic—until it hit your doorstep. But it clearly doesn't matter to you that the unemployment rate for people with disabilities went down during the pandemic. Like, the numbers are startling and the response is comical. Because now people are touting "inclusivity" like they always cared. But now those in power want me to come back to the office. For what? To see me? If you want to see me, in a cubicle that you probably aren't going to go to anyway . . . that double standard is tiring and frankly annoying.

By definition of a capitalistic society, we all have to work. You need money to survive in every part of the world, And in order to get money, you have to work for it—whatever work means to you, right? Because it may not be the labor of going to whatever your job is. But it could be the labor of chasing your benefits. It could be the labor of making the phone calls to get accommodation and care. It could be the labor of filling out the paperwork. It could be the labor of tracking your finances so closely that someone doesn't deposit a gift in your account, putting you over your $2,000 monthly allotment of income for disability insurance. Know that my survival is expensive, and you can't talk to me about equity without talking to me about the price of being Afro-Latina and woman and disabled.

Speaking of which, when is Disability Equal Pay Day? Do you know? Nobody knows or cares to really calculate the data on us, especially broken down by race. We don't talk about Disability Equal Pay Day, not celebrate it. And you know why? Because it's still legal to pay people with disabilities under minimum wage. Solve for that.

At the time this book is being written, the world lost an amazing, courageous activist in Judy Heumann, who once said, "Disability only becomes a tragedy when society fails to provide the things needed to lead one's daily life." The pandemic provides us a real window to see the expertise of those who overcome challenges on a daily basis just to make it to and from hostile work environments. This is not a moment to tout how brave we are to finally be inclusive. This is a moment to reflect as to what made it difficult to begin with, so as not to repeat the same cycle—and to advocate with the disability community who every day, literally, puts its collective body on the line so that each of us can be deemed essential and reasonable.

#CultureChat

- Reflection #1: What does your culture say about your relationship with disabilities, and especially around production, leadership, and accommodations? What are the hurdles those with disabilities are expecting to do on their own just to work? Look at the language around disabilities and support. What stands out to you? How encouraging is the culture around disabilities, including ensuring that disabilities won't hinder equal pay, leadership opportunities, and promotions?
- Reflection #2: What changes or adjustments does your organization need to make around remote work?

While social media has made the realities of police brutality more accessible, the showcasing of brutality toward Black bodies is as old as lynching photos on US postcards. And this brutality is not limited to Black men and boys. The under-showcased harm toward Black women and girls is part of the reason so many fail to mention Breonna Taylor, a Black medical worker whose slumber was disrupted by police officers who opened fire in her apartment. Breonna was killed in March 2020— two months before George Floyd. *Why was the outrage not on the same scale? Why do we forget her name? What makes her different from George Floyd?*

8 | Confront Your Issues with Black Women

I heard in these LinkedIn streets that DEI is not just about being Black. And I heard it came from a person of color. Interesting.

A couple true stories.

■ ■ ■

There was a period in my early thirties where
I was having severe back pain. I worked out
regularly, ate well, and thought I was getting
enough rest. When I got little "ouchies"
here and there, I figured it was from not
stretching enough.
So I invested in all the supportive
ergonomic tools
for both home and office.
Then I incorporated yoga.
And then heating pads when I went to sleep.
Then I brought the heating pad to work.

And then one day at work, as I was typing
my back went out.
My face was on my keyboard.
My peers peeled me back, body still in
ergonomic chair,
Body still bent.
I waited for EMT.
Crying. Balling.
I remember EMT professionals telling me
how they were going to turn me to my side
and get me to the ER.
I was now flat on a stretcher, crying.
Some colleagues ran out of their Capitol
Hill offices.
"Ify, Ify, what's going on? You okay?"
I turned my tear-glossed face away, avoiding
eye contact.
I felt embarrassed.
What am I doing wrong?
Why am I not taking care of myself?
"How are you?" said the doctor.
And with tears, I just ran through all
the things
I had done to take care of myself.
6am workout with Patrice.
Apple and oatmeal for breakfast.
Salad for lunch.
Great posture when I sit,
and sometimes I'll even stand while I type.
He jotted notes as fast as I was rambling,
Pausing only when I took breaths.
And when I had no more to give,
I just stared at the ceiling.

*I hope he believes me. That I'm really taking care
of myself.*

He put his pen down for the first time.

"Ms. Ike, how long has your job been
stressing you out?"

I felt like I was seen for the first time.

And I also felt like I was caught.

Because who cares about Black women dying
slowly at work?

■ ■ ■

When I left the Hill, I went to work for a prestigious nonprofit that does righteous work; to this day, I am both honored to have worked there and in my short time in that role to have made real impact to improve criminal justice. But I also cringe at why I had to leave. I used to say, "No one forced me out, I just had to go for me." But now I realize how flawed even that statement is.

I came back from doing some really cool work, honoring the life and legacy of Nelson Mandela. One of my colleagues asked me if she could come in and catch me up on things. I had been away for a week, so I was ready to be filled in on all the juice. She comes in to share a moment I was really proud of her doing: she approached her boss and laid out the case for why she deserved a promotion and raise. Every kind of "you go, girl" came out of my mouth. That is never easy to do in extremely hierarchical spaces. But then her face changed.

"Ify, you're not gonna believe what he said next."

I stared at her in suspense; with this particular senior director, who happened to be a white man, you just never know what you're going to get.

"He said to me, 'Who put you up to this? Was it Ify?'"

I remember the shock. I stopped eating my watermelon. Another colleague, also a Black woman, walked in my office.

"Oh, I guess you know now," was what she said.

Does the whole office know? And do they know I'm the last to know? What the fuck is happening right now? Why do I feel so ashamed, hurt, betrayed? Why do I want to melt into this wall or run away? Why am I so dark that even when I'm not here, I am?

The day was a blur. I did remember speaking to him, telling him how incredulous it was to me that first, he wouldn't believe that my colleague had the fortitude to demand what she earned on her own; and second, that I could be "blamed" for something *even when I was not even in the vicinity*. I also expressed to him that even if I *had* communicated with her, or any colleague, that his portrayal of me—as somewhat of a puppet master of sorts—was dangerous. Yet, I thanked him for letting me know how he really felt about me, even though I barely spoke to him while in the office. I reminded him that Black women advocating for Black women is not a crime, even if it was all in his imagination.

With the saddest, confused face that begged for sympathy, all he could say was, "Ify . . . I . . . I can't believe this. I am so ashamed of myself. I have so much respect for you and think you are so strong and brilliant. That's why I said what I said."

I knew he didn't get it.

I gave my two-weeks' notice the following week.

But before I left, my back went out again. At work.

■ ■ ■

The harshness of being both Black and a woman wasn't novel to me. Seeing what work was doing to my mother had accustomed me to the expectation that we have to show up and leave our problems at the door. "People will respect you if you do your best." But what happens if the opposite happens? When your best is weaponized? When your best is minimized? When your all is expected, until you pass out.

I started using the term "occupational trauma" right after these moments to best describe what I was experiencing. Prior to that moment, I don't think I had ever determined that any particular event was "traumatizing" for me, though I had witnessed many traumatizing events. But labor and me, me and labor, labor-me, me-labor—we have a complicated relationship. And because part of the relationship with society Black women endure is not being believed, it made sense that I missed the warning signs while at work. It made sense that I began to blame myself. And up until that doctor asked me that question about work, it is quite possible that without that, I may have never disrupted the internal dialogues I had about my labor and my worth.

■ ■ ■

What does "data-informed" mean when you are a Black woman in the workplace?

When I hear that one in two Black women report experiencing racism more at work than anywhere else, I laugh. Not like when I watch *Curb Your Enthusiasm* (I know, I know . . . but it's so funny). The laughter I'm thinking about is more like a smile, like the one Georgina, the Black housekeeper, gives in Jordan Peele's thriller *Get Out*, while shaking her head, saying, "No, no, no, no, no, no." Like Georgina, I knew what it's like to save face while visible and invisible tears flow. I know what it's like when you don't have a choice about showing up for work, even if the day before almost broke you down. In a society that benefits from our need to work due to the intersection of being Black and women and the exponentially greater priorities we hold between work and family, truth—whether from our lips or from research—is not enough. It has never been enough. So other than that data point I've already shared, I'm not sharing any more. Because I don't believe anyone reading this is lost on the data: about our over-qualifications, even as we're underemployed; or the gaslighting we experience when minding our business; or the research on racism being a cause of severe mental illness. That's the funniest research of it all: we needed PROOF that racism kills. Go figure.

You could just believe us and save yourself the peer-review process.

■ ■ ■

So where is the root cause of all this? It's complex as hell and one day, if you're sitting in one of my *African Americans and the Law* classes, you will hear the full chronology of the legal and social significance Black women have to hold to make all this white culture make sense. You will hear the complexities of not being included in the Fifteenth Amendment because you were Black but not a man, but also not being counted as woman enough upon the passage of the Nineteenth Amendment—even after being co-conspirators with white women (who also told us to stand at the back of women's suffrage marches. Thank you, Ida B. Wells, for saying no.). Deeper than the laws that not only obligated enslaved Black women to reserve one of her breasts to be "whites only," is the permanence of our "silent production"; you will suffer the consequences should you dare to push back. And as whiteness is the goal of everyone trying to pursue the American dream, the cries of Black women about our plight and our conditions are hated even by those who also experience oppression but have a different adjacency to whiteness.

This is how a person of color can say with ease, "DEI is not just about being Black."

I won't go into why that is such a ludicrous statement. I'm actually gonna flip it on y'all: What if DEI *was* just about being Black? What if we dared to not see that as a loss, but a collective gain?

You know what is so wild? I think if we all fought for Black women to get equal pay, all women would get it. I think if we all fought for Black disabled persons, it would impact all disabled persons. I think if we all cared about the murder of Black trans women, all LGBTQIA+ youth would be seen.

You see Black women have always been a portal for everyone else's success, even when we're invisible. Imagine what happens when we are visible.

■　■　■

My fellow Black sisters, femme folk, and siblings, I dream of a culture that believes the data; that looks at us the way that doctor looked at me and assesses that the things we describe—and the things we don't yet have the language for—are real. A culture that understands that racism kills and being anti-racist is a requirement. One that doesn't give lip service to our accomplishments but demonstrates they value us by:

1. Honoring and advocating for equal pay as the baseline of our employment.
2. Supporting and encouraging us to take breaks—and give us unlimited time as needed.
3. Providing quality health support, wellness, and mental health support, and creative support in light of the research—the most important being our narratives.
4. Creating pipelines that are not designed to pluck us based on a limited range of standards, like the school we attended, our GPA, the awards we received, the community service that we've done, or our "poverty," "trauma," or "being Black" stories. (The status quo hires all other communities without this extra labor. We deserve to just work and not be a unicorn.)
5. Understanding that sometimes we don't want to be around anyone but each other—because that keeps us safe.
6. Affirming in our workload, evaluations, and performance check-ins that we don't need to be 100 percent all the time, because as humans, that's impossible.
7. Making it the norm to check in with us about the culture, and creating safe spaces for us to report harm.

8. Giving us sabbaticals.

9. Conducting exit interviews that aim not to re-traumatize but to honor our experiences and to document our stories (maybe they'll get it right for the next sister).

10. Holding people accountable who make it hard for us to work, and recognizing that people who aren't able to treat us as full humans don't deserve to be in our space (and probably no one else's).

11. Understanding that while the English language does not always give us the range to describe the discomfort our intuition is sensing about a space, that does not invalidate what we know to be true about the harm we are experiencing.

What else should be on this list, Fam?

■ ■ ■

Like I said, I'm not gonna try to convince you with data. I'm gonna share three short excerpts that I shared at different moments on LinkedIn. Jot down what comes to you.

There's a difference between "listen to Black women" and "be led by Black women."

Many of our organizational spaces have room to hear us and even congratulate our achievements. But to be led by a sistah is a different story. Especially if she's focused on doing her job, not making you comfortable.

Serious questions to ponder:

Black women have opinions. Does that make you mad sometimes?

Black women have a full set of human emotions. Which ones bother you?

Black women have a range of tones and voices and delivery methods. Which ones make you frustrated, nervous, or even scared?

Most Black women have endured occupational trauma before they met you. Do you think of that during your interactions with us, especially when there's conflict or tensions?

I actually care how you process these questions. Healthy leaders confront their own ways of being, and are open to "maybe it's me, not them." Because as fancy as we'd like to make our PowerPoints and presentations, some of y'all have a Black women issue when we don't appear to you a certain way. And it's impacting our collective progress.

Something to really consider this Women's History Month.

■ ■ ■

Improving the conditions of those with intersectional lives requires intentionality that may make some uncomfortable, including challenging which marginalized voices we tend to favor—and which ones we continue to exclude.

Are darker-hued Black women and femme folk included when looking for experts?

Full bodied?

How about shorter-haired, kinky-haired, coils, or braids?

And what about our femme peers of color who are more introverted?

Or opinionated?

Or got more bass in their voice, muscle in their arms, or an accent?

And do any or all of the above have to be extra nice for your comfort?

This depth deserves time and space in our equity dialogues.

■ ■ ■

I am a Black woman,
And yes that's my rate.

#CultureChat

1. Look at your recruitment, promotion, leadership, and attrition data. Do you track women based on race? If so, what are the trends as they relate to Black women within your organization? If not—why don't you (and you should)?

2. Do you have a sense of what Black women's experiences have been within your organization? How did you become aware of that information?

3. Does your organization suffer from the "unicorn" syndrome (hiring only exceptional people, especially as it relates to Black women and other people of color)? What does that say about your selection process?

4. Do your HR policies have a process for handling racial aggressions within the organization, including but not limited to mental health days, coverage for therapy, and/or compensatory relief?

5. If your organization does culture training, how many sessions are dedicated to intersectionality and specifically misogynoir (the unique combination of racism and sexism experienced by Black women)?

6. Are there programs intentionally preparing Black women to be in senior leadership, in accordance with the data that reveals that Black women—more than any of their counterparts—desire to be in senior leadership?

7. What are the standards of beauty and professionalism within the organizations? Are there trends that you have for Black women?

8. Are you uncomfortable managing Black women? If so, why?

Final thoughts:

- If you have Black women in your organization, and you desire to hear their insights, consider doing so with a facilitator or guide. It is not always safe for us to share the unhealthy aspects of our environments—and the people within them.
- List all the areas where the organization needs to improve in relation to Black women across the work life cycle stages (recruitment, hiring, promotion, exit) and actionable steps in each of those areas on a committed time schedule.
- If your organization does not have Black women in leadership, understand why that is. Identify internal and external pipelines to shift that, recognizing that all of the culture, diversity, and equity issues do not rest in their laps.
- Colorism is very real and a byproduct of colonialism, white dominant culture, and slavery. Please read the study about how women experience differences in society and the workplaces, including the Catalyst study,[1] which assessed the experiences of those within multiple marginalized identities, examining racism, skin tone bias and colorism, texturism, cissexism, and heterosexism.[2]
- Remember, Black women don't have to be good all the time.

9

The Case for Radical Sabbaticals

Problem Statement: In Pursuit of Rest

From the Crown Act to the notion of the "strong Black woman," Western cultures' infatuation with glaring at the bodies, features and selective (survival) behaviors of Black women demonstrate the hyper-visible experiences—reduced often to "exotic" parts of our humanity, or the parts that can be commercialized, exploited, and targeted. But systemic racism also invisiblizes the full impact of the "strong Black woman" trope; until movies like *12 Years a Slave*, mass culture had not fully appreciated the exhausting existence of an enslaved girl or woman, who often not only had to work as hard as their male counterparts in the day, but also faced normalized sexual brutality from slave owners—and physical and psychological abuse from slave owner's wives. Compared with other women in the United States, Black women have always had the highest labor participation. In 1880, 35.4 percent of married Black women and 73.3 percent of single Black women were in the labor force. This is in comparison to just 7.3 percent of married white women and 23.8 percent of single white women. As white women typically left the labor market after marriage, Black women continued to work over the course of their full lives—an extension of the devaluation of Black women as mothers and their own caregiving needs at home. It is worth noting that most Black women had to take on the role of co-breadwinners, as blatant discriminatory practices towards Black men meant the survival of the Black family relied on both partners working underwaged jobs, with Black women historically holding low-wage agriculture and domestic service positions—even after the "Great Migration" to the north during the 20th century.

Although white communities devalued Black women as mothers to their own children, Black women have been—and remain—the most likely of all women to be employed in low-wage domestic jobs that involve cooking, cleaning, and care giving. This generational burden of being all things to all people, not having enough for yourself or your family—all while racism and bias deprive Black women from spending that equal amount of time at home—is a normalized reality within our society.

The desire to keep Black women tied to labor to ultimately benefit whiteness is further evidenced by reviewing laws intended to support mothers. The welfare policies of the early twentieth century, including statewide Mother's Pensions and the national passage of the Social Security Act of 1935 (later renamed the Aid to Families with Dependent Children) were designed to enable poor, and often single, white mothers to stay home and provide care for their children. As Deborah Gray White's book *Making a Way Out of No Way* reveals, caseworkers systematically excluded most poor Black women from receiving cash assistance up until the 1960s, expecting Black women to remain employed while being mothers and depriving them of the chance of being at home.[3] As data emerged about the disparities between Black and white families as a result of these policies, Black women gradually were accepted into the program. But very quickly, attitudes around the program shifted, and now the once supportive program, which white mothers enjoyed, was seen as an "entitlement program" once Black women participated. Much of these attitudes could be seen within the naming of subsequent policies. The Personal Responsibility and Work Opportunity Reconciliation Act, also known as the Welfare Reform Bill of 1996, thus ended the Aid to Families with Dependent Children (AFDC) and replaced it with the Temporary Assistance for Needy Families program (TANF). The former law guaranteed benefits to all recipients whose income and resources were below federally guided, state-determined eligibility levels. TANF, however, gave states the authority to determine eligibility requirements and benefit levels. Another major shift: strict work requirements were now connected to the distribution of most TANF benefits. These seemingly race-neutral policies, coupled with employment discrimination, have resulted in Black mothers with school-age children being more likely to be in the labor force (78 percent of Black mothers, compared to 66 percent of white, Asian, and Latinx mothers), and surviving on a median annual income of just over $43,209, compared to $67,629 annually for white, non-Hispanic men. The double theft of safety net programs and wages has a real impact on the stability of Black families and communities, since 80 percent of Black mothers are breadwinners in their families. That's over 4 million families.[4]

Not Designed to Rest: How Rest Is Not a Real "Choice" for Many Black Women

The foundation of discrimination towards Black women is a shared abuse whether a woman has biological children or not—as evidenced by the lack of focus and investment in workplace exploitation. The advancement of the New Deal, the praised social reform package of President Franklin D. Roosevelt had several exclusions that harmed Black people, and Black women in particular: minimum wage, overtime pay and collective bargaining measures excluded sectors Black women worked, including domestic service. States were not incentivized to extend full worker protections to Black women, a practice which exists to this day. Black women are still overly concentrated in lower-waged industries, which tend to be inflexible, and lack health insurance, paid sick and maternity leave and paid vacations. Over a third of Black women workers lack paid sick leave.

COVID-19 revealed another phenomenon: even when such benefits are provided, Black women *still* can't afford to leave the workplace. According to the Center for American Progress (CAP), in a given year the majority of Black women do not take leave for parental, caregiver, or personal health needs. For those who need to, about 42 percent of those leaves are taken without pay. It is estimated that Black women lose about $3.9 billion each year due to lost wages while on health, parental, or caregiver leave. This doesn't even account for loss of wages due to unemployment as a result of taking leave, which means these figures are actually higher. These losses harm the majority of Black families, further contributing to collective insecurity, and the deeper widening of health disparities disproportionately experienced by Black women.[5] It is worth noting that one in three Black women worked frontline jobs during the pandemic, putting them and their families at higher risk of infection. But, unfortunately, too many Black women did not have a real choice to rest and recover, or stay at home to prevent exposure to COVID.

Persistent employment discrimination is a factor for Black women across economic realities. Despite all the renewed focus on diversity, equity, and inclusion practices at companies after the 2020 murder of George Floyd, Black women continue to experience racism and micro-aggressions[6] in the workforce, including higher-waged environments. The annual "Women in the Workplace"[7] report highlights the many regular occurrences Black women experience while working, including hearing people express "surprise" at their language skills, intellect, or ability; a disconnect between DEI programs and actual culture changes to alleviate aggressions and stressors; and under-promotions to managerial and senior positions. Burnout and stress also continue to impact Black women differently while in the workplace, especially as they are seeking jobs that better meet their family and health needs. According to research from the National Women's Law Center, Black women's unemployment (5.8 percent) has been significantly higher than that of white, Asian, and Latinx women.[8]

Beyond Paid Leave: A "Case for Black Women Leave" to Be Beyond (and Disconnected) from Work

For Black women to survive with full lives, a major disruption to the status quo has to occur. The cycle of exhaustion is one which is embedded in the fabric of this culture:

1. White-dominant culture is designed to maintain the original intention of racialized capitalism, which has serious implications for the quality of life for Black women, who are doubly suppressed by chattel slavery and patriarchy.
2. "Work culture" is an extension of slave practices, and thus the expectations around Black women and labor are of high output with very little return to the worker.
3. Black women are expected to lead transformative movements that center the lives of Black people and women. Yet there have been zero mass movements that center the wellness, liberation, and rest of Black women.
4. Black women have been pouring at half-full for generations, to the enjoyment of everyone but them. Even to get rest, they must prove they "deserve" it.

5. Black women are experiencing an isolating and silenced exploitation period, especially having inherited chronic discrimination and ongoing pandemics, with inadequate recovery time or resources.

6. Rest as a movement is a revolutionary act because it would cause every system to quantify the contributions of Black femme labor, and to evaluate what would need to change.

In the medical field, the principle of *rest and recovery* (also called the *principle of recuperation*) suggests that rest and recovery from the stress of exercise must take place in proportionate amounts to avoid too much stress, and thus breakdown of the body. The conversation around the health disparities Black women face, from death while birthing to overexposure to racism, is pretty commonplace. What is not common is seeing *rest and recovery* as necessary for Black bodies to live and thrive.

Our theory of change is simple: increase the frequency of rest and recovery, in the form of radical sabbaticals for Black women and other marginalized femme folks—regardless of industry one is in—in the hopes of reducing the impact of economic, political, and social stressors and increasing the length and quality of their lives. By increasing the conversation, practice, and praxis around this work, we can finally create a strategy to respond to the inhumane expectations built around Black femme labor.

Meet L. Toni Lewis, M.D. (she/her), President and Founder of Liberation Health Strategies

The fires we are forced to put out daily take up the space of us getting a chance to just breathe, rest, create.

The default cycle of "extraction, exploitation, work them into the ground" doesn't create the space for imagination. Some of the best and brightest ideas are held deep in the souls of folks who innovate every day, in their budgets, figuring out how to get the kids to school and college with a dime and a slice of bread, or folks like me. I would love to have nothing to do, but think and play with infinite capital.

From our very core, there's this battle that's going on that doesn't always give us the space for imagination and then when you keep working with the communities we take care of, because if you are a workforce healthcare person more than likely you're not just that at the job, you're that for the family, you're that for the block, for the church, etc.

And then for the folks who have some privilege and space, you know, the courage to let their egos go and allow kind of some of that genius to rise and to try shit, like, innovate and invest and fund like you would fund a white tech boy trying to get plastic out of the ocean. Why does it have to be so hard?

As a practitioner in the field of medicine, I'm often asked, "What needs to shift for things to be more equitable for people of color?" And my response is: there's culturally connected and then there is a cultural connection to the doctrine and there must be an understanding that the doctrine can shift. If you're a medical professional who has simply memorized what the textbooks held, there won't automatically be a connection to the community. Exposure to the community and asking questions, you realize that the more you learn, the more you need to learn. You gotta stay curious, listen, and remain open. You can't even get to a plan or diagnosis unless you really know the history of what's going on with the person.

Believe You Deserve It All

By Ember Phoenix (They/She), Healer and Strategist

Liberation principles can absolutely be infused into equitable culture design work. My work is my purpose. I think the issue with the current social dynamic is that people work because they're forced to work. And it's why we have this discontent with like, this new generation that's like, "*I'm not fucking working, like, I'm gonna do nothing, just hand me something!*" They need a little bit of help with understanding that it's not about not working, but it's about being in your purpose with the work you're doing and having that benefit community. That said, that disruption is also liberating how we connect the need to survive with the ways society forces us to take just any condition because we have to work.

I am a healer. I am now working for a nonprofit. Before I worked for this nonprofit, I was working for myself, because I stopped working for corporations and stopped working with people who did not value my time and my labor. As a Black human, I'm good at almost anything I do. And if it matters enough to me, I make myself good at it even if I don't like it. And so I was basically doing work that a supervisor was doing, but getting paid as a menial employee and kept getting work piled on me. But if I got too smart or too bright, you know, I'd get pushed down in the work field because I'm Black, and I can't be that. So they wanted my labor, but they wanted to use my brilliance—but they did not want to highlight or honor my brilliance.

This leaves many stuck: there's not a thing we can do but show up in support of a system that is broken. The system has to change, but that system doesn't want to change. So I left the system and found a way to do that healing elsewhere. It was not an easy thing, and it was not a comfortable thing. It is a very lonely and a very scary thing. But at the end of the day, the way I knew I had to leave the system was that I couldn't sleep at night. I knew that I was causing harm, and although it was the fault of the system, it did not change the harm I was causing to others and to myself. And I was thinking about my grandmother, who was a midwife who died because she did too much due to ancestral trauma, where Black women have been taught that they need to martyr themselves and sacrifice themselves for the greater good. She was my heart. She was everything to me and she was Cherokee, she was Indigenous, so a part of her knew better. And yet, it was the grind. Everything she was, was for us. She didn't care about herself. She had the mentality of her grandmother and her great grandmother—that mentality that it doesn't matter what happens to self, just make it better for the next generation. That is a trope that keeps cycles going.

Until we get into the mindset where we realize we deserve it all and stop letting little tiny wins be enough and keep pushing with that same amount of force to get what we really deserve. We are holding so much and we don't believe we deserve: but we deserve. And until we shift our mindset, we're not going to change drastically enough to make a difference because these systems took way too long to get in place and that little chipping away isn't going to do anything because while we're chipping, they're rebuilding; they're fortifying.

If you truly care about equity, that may mean looking at whether or not you're the wrong person in the position that you're in or whether or not you need to be willing to start all the way over outside of the current system and build something different.

10 | Safety, Access, and a Good Sandwich

#EquityMindset with Dominique Morgan

(grab some tea, a blanket, and make sure you have some time)

> Dominique Morgan (she/her) is an artist, award-winning activist, and the inaugural Fund for Trans Generations' Program Director at Borealis Philanthropy. She is the former executive director of Black and Pink National, an organization that provides support to incarcerated queer persons.

Ify: Okay, so you look fabulous! Let me flip my braids to the side so I can give a little something!

Dominique: Listen, I don't play with my hair, and I don't play with my purses.

Ify: Well, you never play, and I'm so happy you're here today. You were the first to respond to my invite to chat about this, so let's just open up with what equity mindset means to you and what does that mean for you as an individual and for communities that you support?

Dominique: You know, I bring a couple of thoughts and perspectives as a former executive director, who ran a multimillion-dollar national nonprofit, having a staff of 25 across the country with most of that growth happening in the pandemic. I'm also thinking about that question from the perspective of being someone who was formerly incarcerated and needed access to employment that would position me to be successful in a multi-definition approach of success. And now I work in philanthropy where, you know, I'm navigating what still feels like ridiculous amounts of money. And I'm thinking about access to people. Equity historically translates to access. If equity is in place, there's rarely a barrier to access. When I got your email about this, that's what really resonated with me because that's the type of work that I care about. It's not just about, "Can Dominique get on the other side," but it's the sort of other side that anybody can get to if they want that.

When we started this conversation talking about hair and stuff, as a Black trans woman, presentation oftentimes equals safety for me. And depending on how great my presentation is, it can lead to me being more unsafe than being safe, especially depending on how much my presentation results in cisgendered men finding me attractive, right. But in the same sense, there are different things that contribute to that safety and equity, too. This wig is a $1,000 wig. It's not a brag, it's a "me wearing this hair, masked up, no makeup or whatever, it gives an effect, it brings me a sense of safety." Now some people are like, "Girl, I want locs, I want a Dora Milaje, bald head moment," and all that's wonderful, girl, for you. But for me, when I think of what equity looks like, it's for every Black trans woman who thinks that this sort of wig and this sort of hairstyle would make her feel safer to be able to experience that and either be affirmed or say, "You know what, I don't want it anymore."

When equity goes wrong, I think, is when we feed into communities, especially marginalized communities that only some people deserve access. As a result, we spend our whole lives wanting that access. And the gag is that there are some of us who once we've had the privilege of access and experienced equality, usually through the ladder of tokenism, we get on the other side of it, and come back and minimize that access and be like, "Oh, girl, I had that. It wasn't all that and I divest from it." And then we judge people who want to steal, but we don't hold that they want to steal because they never had the chance to have "the thing" to even decide if they want it anymore or don't.

So that was a bit of a rant, but that's what your question on equity mindset translates to, especially in the space of employment, meaning economy: we live in a world where literally not everyone can grind it out. No matter how hard you grind, some will grind in the spaces where they need to be grinding. I can never really look around and be like, "Oh my god, I'm really all that." But some really believe that about themselves. You are great, but you're not the greatest. Because some people, if they got a chance to get where you were, the girls would sit you down. But because of the way these systems are set up, some of us get to sit in spaces and flourish, believe we're the greatest ever, and drink the Kool-Aid, which perpetuates every other system that keeps us held back in my opinion.

Ify: What you just said around "you're great, but you're not the greatest" is actually very grounding and humbling as a practitioner and a great reminder. I'm doing my best, and I can do great work. But also there are people that are even more on the margins than I am that are also greater than I am, even if they don't have access to the things that I have. And that doesn't bring fear, but humility. And also several opportunities for us to live our full purpose in this equity work, and not emulate another practitioner or feel the need to perform. But I can imagine that there are times where people feel guilty doing this work, either for their performance, or fear of not meeting the needs of another co-worker or colleague. What are some of the ways that people can break through their guilt to actually get toward a place of problem solving?

Dominique: I would offer that the calling isn't to *not* feel the guilt, it's to not let the guilt hold you hostage. Because I think with guilt there's an ebb and flow and different words that surround guilt. I think there's a certain space and range that at times goes to sadness and then at other times goes to shame. There's a lot that surrounds the ecosystem of guilt. And you want to feel it, but the work is to not let that be where you stop the process.

I'm just coming off a surgery, and I am not a workout doll. And I'm trying to learn this whole "walking and doing activities" thing all over again. And it's kind of like, you know, you remember running the mile as a teenager, and you would kind of stop midway through, right? And it's like, "Okay, stop and rest," yes, but don't let that be where you stop. And sometimes the "stopping" is because folks who do not have experience with the full experience of Black intersectional lives are connected not to our lives, but to their emotions in reaction to our lives. So they stop at their "oh my God" when they even see me because what they're thinking about is who I am or how hard it must be for me. And then they want to tell me how sad they are about my life. In a TED Talk I did several years ago, I talked about resilience: I don't want to be celebrated just for being resilient. The thing that was supposed to kill me but didn't; I don't want that to be the only accolade I have. Because people will only navigate you in that way. And there's a certain type of response they expect from me in that space. Almost like an appreciation for their sympathy. Now here's the flip side of that, though. The flip side of it, though, is that when you get to the point where you know who you are, and it's not based on their sympathy or how they move in that guilt, then they get afraid of you—you're too boisterous. You now become "a lot."

But let me also be transparent because I challenge myself to also not sit in guilt. Me being a Black trans woman in the United States, multi-degreed, who owns a home, multiple cars, has a title, makes over

six figures—I'm naming all those things to say I'm
instantly one of the most affluent Black trans women
in this country, in this world. In this country and
perhaps in this world, right? That's just the truth. The
last time I saw you was when you were training at
the Creating Change Conference, and as I'm talking
to my sisters in community, 99 percent of the girls
that I spoke to shared that I have more than them.
Add to that the number of times that I get a call that
another Black trans girl is gone. And I'm like, "God,
why am I still here?" So I have to feel it. But then
through that, as you said, I need to switch to "Okay,
what, what am I able to do? Why do I feel guilty?
Why am I questioning my permanence, my existence through these kinds of identities? Why am I
always drawing the lucky card?" I can name all of
that. You gotta name it And then it's like, "Well, what
do I do with the luck I have? And how am I connected authentically to people?" If you feel that
guilty, are they able to let you know how you can be
of service to them?

I think it's slightly toxic to be able to look at a
community like, "Oh my God, I feel so bad." You
have a good cry, wash your face, and get up and go,
but you don't have the proximity for them to reach
you and tell you what they need. I had a person
today say, "Hey, Dominique, I need to put you down
and say you were my former manager at this job."
Yeah, go ahead, put me down. Because I know when
I email "Dominique Morgan" from my job, they are
never going to question me. People may not like
that, but that is me using my power and influence
for a young Black woman with her child to be able

to have access to a job; that don't hurt me at all whatsoever. I've maybe lied about more for less, Hello! I think that through that searching and investigation of your guilt, you find all the ways you can show up. And as Black folks, showing up can be hard. But I have never experienced a love that is more true, that is more consistent, that satiates me more than a Black person in a space of power, who has used their power, sometimes to put me on, and other times to get out the way. And that's how I try to move.

Ify: You are providing so many different practical practices that people can utilize, literally for free. But I also recognize that some of this should not be free. So let's get to equity, as in coins. When we talk about the economy, specifically for Black and Brown trans women, the data is incomplete, to say the least. We also limit the conversation to not talk beyond survival. Our society doesn't center any discussions about our trans community's future: what it looks like from a space of wellness. Add to that, that children, trans youth, are being punished before they even fully start their journeys. Like adults using their full power, to snuff out another human's journey. Much of this equity mindset is exploring some of the broad practices we need to employ, but equity is also about knowing how to be intentionally specific about the needs of communities experiencing unique disparities. You've used the word "safety" multiple times, which signals to me that "equity and safety" are married—there is no one without the other. So what does that look like, specifically, from early education to pipeline to mentorship to sponsorship? My sense is we need some specific things, and in abundance. That said, I want to recognize that just because communities are marginalized, it doesn't mean that abundance doesn't exist within our spaces, right?

Dominique: I think, for me, the safety and equity conversation, at the root, is connected to both access to financial stability and the ability to control my actual self, my body. For example, as a Black trans woman traveling, it's like me traveling with Precheck, with Clear is a very different experience than a Black trans woman walking through TSA, having to get patted down. It's different. And for some people, they may feel like, "Well, it's a small investment to get those protections," but it costs. Me sitting in first class, even if a white woman doesn't "live" for me, she's going to treat me differently because of that. Some people are hearing this and saying, "Oh my God, that's a capitalist mindset." Well, I live in a capitalist society. You cannot shame me for playing, learning, and wanting to figure out the game so that I'm all right. We need an abundance of understanding on that front.

We are also communicating at a time where all of these bills are being passed that are not only embedded with fear, they hurt us all, but we're not even hip to it as a society. Tennessee just passed this bill banning drag performance. But what people aren't realizing is that while it's discussing people who are perceived to be another gender based on how they dress publicly, this will lead to not establishing new standards, but actually re-establishing laws that have existed to address the trans experience in our community. CPAC [the Conservative Political Action

Conference], the biggest, most powerful space for Republicans to come and talk, Michael Knowles and others talked about eradicating "transgenderism" in our communities. Like our existence is some new phenomenon. And I say those things because it actually isn't about a political ideology. This is about the truth and facts of our bodies not being counted; we don't count trans people in the census. So people will act like we just showed up yesterday. We most likely won't be added to the census because now, our lives are being framed as an agenda and the response will be, "Y'all tryna push this on us." And Black folks, too; we need to not be regurgitating these talking points created in white spaces because these talking points are also trying to establish a norm of invalidating us as Black people—that's a gag.

And much of this "Where did they come from?" blowback stems from trans folks who are just trying to live and enter the workforce; be employed and get financial access. Right now, so many cannot walk into your McDonald's and be hired and say, "Hi, my name is Dominique," and be respected even if my name tag or ID says something else. So then what happens? These girls are becoming TikTok famous. These girls are becoming Instagram famous. These girls are starting Only Fans accounts. These girls are taking non-traditional ways to get access to financial support, not because they're like, "Oh my God, I want to spend 10 hours a day making TikToks." But because I can't go into UPS, get hired and make my overtime. And you need overtime to protect our lives, Baby. I am a lifelong Nebraskan; I moved to Atlanta eight months ago. What I know is no matter where I go, this space is safe. But it costs me a lot of money per month to ensure that no matter what is happening out there in the world, I have this space that is mine. That's what trans folks, specifically trans folks of color are trying to fight for. So if there is no equity and access to financial security—which historically also speaks to physical safety—then we are inherently setting up trans folks to die in this society. And that goes to the pipeline conversation.

And I just want to name that we know those are the same ways that they set up Black cis women to be eradicated, and Black cis men to be eradicated: the same systems are happening, and it's impacting how we see each other. So you asked, "What should people be doing?" I want to start with us first. Mariame Kaba opened up a conversation with the concept of a "grace potion" to me. When I see Black cis women online who are very publicly angry about Black trans women, I don't perceive that those sisters hate me. I perceive those sisters have been through so much shit that they're in the words of Effie White in *Dreamgirls*, "What about me?" Like, what happened? How'd you leave me out here? How do I not matter? And I think equity speaks to us creating spaces for folks to deal with what they went through. We should be doing everything we can to think of and with the design question of "What does love, care, and restoration look like?" Listen this equity thing, equity is a lot of work, because you can't just go forward, right? You got to look forward, and I look back, look right, look to the side.

None of us are capable of doing this singularly. I may only have the capacity to look forward. So I gotta have you, Sis, and be like "Sis, you got my back," "Bro, can you get me here," "Fam, can you look this way to see if I'm missing something?" And I gotta do the same. If we are not dedicated to naming the systems that we survived while making sure those systems do not continue to harm, then what are we doing? I need to be just as mad at how the system is treating you and hold grace at times as to why you may not be able to see me in the process.

I'm in a program at Stanford that talked about how worthless empathy is because for most, empathy is the tactic of hearing someone and trying to find where their story sits in yours. And it's all of this mirroring. They offered that it's about compassionate care, with a definition that compassion is looking at one's pain, harm, or difficult things and just sitting in it. Being with it. Like really appreciating what that thing is doing to a human being—without how it makes you feel. And I believe that's where equity needs to start. And that's a skill we need to be better at. You got to be able to look at something and sit in the hardness and the ugliness of it, feel it. And then be strategic. The girls don't know how to do a SWOT [strengths, weaknesses, opportunities, and threats] analysis, no more, no shade, right? Thinking critically and with complexity and nuance—that is the only way to be effective. Now if you just want to do something to be cute and you don't want to be effective, then my goodness, continue to do so. As a member of the world of philanthropy, these are the questions I ask my colleagues every day: "What are we doing?" And as a Black trans woman who is dedicated to access, and looking at my own privilege as well as the privilege of those around me—I am not excited to be the only one in the room; that does not move me. So part of that pipeline is understanding how others are surviving and being open to hearing how they no longer want to be ignored and forgotten. That's important.

Ify: As you're speaking, I'm sitting here really sitting with something. It's not even guilt, maybe it's anger, but like angered into a desire for action. You know, in the Black community, we say all the time, "We got us." Sometimes, we frame it as "we all we got." So as I'm speaking to you about pipelines, I'm like, "Dominique is someone's mentor, someone's sponsor." Like, we got that! Yes, we deserve access to traditional entry points into the workplace and ladders to positions of power. But let's not abandon the wealth we have within our community, as a people. Like, as we heal, we open up pipeline support. We become each other's sponsors, and it stems from not turning away from each other's journeys, but activating from that compassionate care. We can activate the "community of the oppressed" and get stronger by seeing our experiences in each other, and being like, "Let me help you, because they tried that shit with me too."

Dominique: And also because you asked a question earlier about what are the abundant things we have in our community. Grab a pen, this is a prompt for you, this is "free game," and I want to attend a session where you walk us through this question: "Give me a solution that does not depend on my oppressor giving me permission to enact it." You feel how long that pause is? Because that's what I do every day. As someone who was formerly incarcerated, people are always like, "Dominique, how did you manage?" I lived in a world where the people who locked me in my cell, I would have to ask them for toilet paper. And depending on the C.O., no matter how terrible they were to me, if I did not use a term they liked, they were not going to give me toilet paper. But if I sat there and used the bathroom on myself, I would be put in segregation. Learning what it takes to ask your oppressor for freedoms taught me that I'm always looking for the solutions where I don't ever have to ask somebody—where I can get that thing they don't want me to have in the first place. When I do that, that usually means I am depending on community solutions for change. And that means I'm spending more time with Black folks. And those are the moments when I'm like, "Oh, dang, my home girl got all of these skills. Girl, let me celebrate you," and two, "Do other folks know about this?" and three, "Let me pay you. How do I get you paid?" And we do that within our spaces. When I depend on community solutions for change—when I lean into solutions that do not require my oppressor to give me the green light—I am historically wrapped in the most powerful Black beautiful moments.

Like I am having vivid conversations of abolition and systems-free responses. I live in Atlanta where these conversations of "cop cities" are happening. I was talking to someone today, and I said, if somebody was kicking in my door right now, I know that my brother Malcolm will get here from Decatur,

Georgia, in 90 minutes quicker than the police will get here. And he'll be concerned about making sure I'm safe, first. For the folks who live for the police experience, God bless you. I just have done the work to know my people well enough to see their strengths. I am dedicated to seeing it, affirming it, naming it and being rooted in it.

As a Black trans woman, my blackness and my transness is never more powerful than when I'm in a room with Black people. And I do not want to live in a world where I don't get to feel powerful. I do not want to live in a world where I don't know the cheat code to get to my powerful space. And I don't want to live in a world where once I've understood my power, figured out the cheat code to get to my powerful space, that I'm not doing the work for other people to know their power, know the cheat codes and be there with me.

Ify: My hope for this project is, in part, for people to be curious about other frameworks and other people's processes and then get out their notebooks and walk into new possibilities for social design. Just building this muscle for all that is there, and much of what we've missed, but was always there. For me lately, I find myself listening more to Toni Morrison interviews now that she has transitioned, than when she was here. I'm thinking specifically of fellow Jersey girl, Marsha P. Johnson and really thinking about "Have we really sat with her words?" Not just the very public, heroic act of disruption, but also like the philosophy of a brilliant human being? Or like the Cohambee River Collective's stance on not just inclusion, but militancy. Like fighting for all Black femme folk to be liberated as an opening to human liberation. In my personal circles, we call it a queer politic. And when I think about equity, I don't [know] how equity could not encompass that. And I say that both in intimate settings, but within organizations that put out these mission statements shortly after our lives are brutalized and trivialized across every form of digital platform. I wonder what if they even know that that is a design moment? A framework moment? A shifting space? A time to get lost in dialogue outside of their own.

And also what it would take for there to be more queer folk of color, more Black queer folk to be in leadership, right? Even though leadership pipelines also force us to wear the corporate mask at times, which stifles creative solution making. One of my clients is a Black queer C-suite leader, and I asked him what it would feel like for his team to be fully free. And, you know he was sharing stuff. And, honestly, I was bored. It was basic, and I knew it wasn't him So I asked him, "Are you bringing your full self to this question? Like your full beautiful, bold, creative, Beyoncé-loving self?" And something clicked, Dominique. His description, from what I remember, had raindrops in it. And he started describing the movement of his team—he's a dancer—and how he'd bring that experience of a dancer into the future of work. And he started describing the ways he would want his team members to see his critique as supportive as Debbie Allen . . .

Dominique: Oh! Okay, now . . .

Ify: Right! You see what you just did? A whole posture change when you hear that. And I got it, I got the vision, and I wished that for him and his team. Whatever these textbooks taught us about leadership, that's not actually working. And also, what works for you in real life doesn't have to be totally outside of the workplace. But I also know that's the way we've been conditioned.

Dominique: My response to this narrative is based on how you just made me feel. Because it sits in spirit more than in process. Because those shoulders that hit, bam, and rise up and head back, like so. That is a very Black thing; that shot something up in me. Because when you say, "Debbie Allen," I said, "Oh, boy, shattah!" like I know that. And not even from a space of religiosity. I'm saying spirit is a power that is outside of yourself, that is moving. When there's equity, there is freedom, there is liberation. And check the process and ways of being that got to that: you asked a very simple question and then followed up with a big question that created so much space for these people and that made me think about how we think and what we place value on. An equity mindset in this world is me feeling like I can learn from everything and that my growing does not feel inequitable, either. Baby, I want to learn something watching a Marvel show, baby! When *WandaVision* said, "But what is grief if not love persevering?" I screamed "Mercy!" You got to be open, though, you got to be open. And there's some people in our world who are so open that they get made fun of. I want to live in a world where the most open people are the people we look up to. Because in that, it means that I have created so much capacity, my lens has shifted so much to where I see an opportunity to address my epistemology so often that there is inherent safety there. You are a world-class coach. People who learn from you are open and feel safe in a space.

And last but not least, it's a space where we respect all of what it takes to get to the culture we deserve; we can't cherry-pick what it takes to get us to equity. It's the whole shebang or it's not. You know, I worked in New York for several months last year. And you know, y'all out there on the East Coast make some sandwiches that you'd be like, "Girl, I want to eat this." They be the most sloppiest sandwiches. But it's fire. You cannot have just the parts, baby, but everything. And I think this work is messy. This is difficult. It's complicated. You gotta roll up your sleeves, you better have a bunch of napkins, but lean in. You know that "sandwich hunch," when you lean into it . . .

Ify: Yes that hunch! 'Cuz you don't want nothing to fall out, no onions . . .

Dominique: There's an intentionality, Sis! You can't eat that sandwich haphazardly, 'cuz you gonna lose a piece. That type of engagement is what it takes for equity to happen. And when you walk into a restaurant and you see people eating. Some people is hunching. And some people is just tasting. Baby, be a huncher, Amen!

Ify: Ashe!

Dominique: And I gotta repeat before we close: folks have to be okay, hell, even happy, being "great" and divesting from wanting to be "the greatest." That is the key. And lastly, and I will shut up after this: Black trans women and Black cisgender women, I want us to recognize that we do not exist in a full joyful experience without each other. That is not me saying we don't exist without each other. That is not me discussing whether the chicken or the egg came first. I'm not getting into that. I'm saying "Ify, my sister, I am not better off if you are not here." And I mean that shit. I mean that. If we do not do that, if that is not a part of your equity mindset as a Black femme in this world, you will be caught up in the masculine gaze; the masculine power will catch you up every time.

11

What Is Your Equity (Mindset) Journey?

The newness of making our spaces more equitable may make the concept seem too big or unapproachable. Even as a practitioner, I find myself needing a moment to ask myself, *Why does this matter to me?* Some of my response lies within the ways equity played in my life—or more accurately the ways I desired for it to be present. Other parts of my response emerge from the spaces where I watched inequity manifest in other people's lives. Part of accepting our calling as equity designers is having a close relationship with how we got here. I have found that many of these moments have also helped me forgive the parts of me that used to think I was the problem. If asked, "What is your equity journey?" what parts of your life would stick out? here's a sneak into some of the journeys in my life that have shaped my understanding of the world we inherited.

Where Are the Swings?

Desiring equity was always real for me as a young child, even if I didn't know it. I didn't know why Mommy and Daddy were out of the house for such long hours for this thing they called "work," but I did know I wanted more time with each of them—both individually and as a family unit. That feeling hasn't left to this day, but hey, kids adjust, right? I recall me and my sister memorizing the fake address (68 Ray Street) we needed to share to administrators at our elementary school because we lived in the city of Trenton, New Jersey, about 10 minutes from the school in the township of Ewing. My parents never said, "These are the better schools," but I put the puzzle pieces together from internal and external message: my hood isn't good enough to get a good education; life is about constantly positioning myself for success 'cause no one is coming to save me; and if you don't want to fall behind, then this all comes at a cost.

The earliest cost was sleep. To this day, my internal clock wakes up at the same time since age five, around 6:00 a.m. Not sure how we were so efficient that early in the morning; then all five of us were getting ready, with one bathroom, for school, work, and Head Start. In those days, we had to eat breakfast in the car while one of our parents drove us over to the fake address (which was my uncle's home) early enough to make it seem like we were coming out of the house and waiting for the bus like other kids. After two great years at a school with the biggest school playground I'd ever played on, we were called to the principal's office, my sister and me. And surprisingly, there was my dad, who had to rush over from work. They basically told us the jig was up, that they knew we were not residents of the township, and that we had to leave immediately or face repercussions. My dad and the administrators go back and forth while me and my sister strain our necks, looking up at the giants battling it out. But I knew what was happening; our carriage turned into a pumpkin. Afternoons once filled with hands in the air whizzing down yellow slides or hanging from jungle gyms—all on soft wood chips and mulch, were now filled with a vacant lot at my new school. I remember at age seven asking, *Where are the swings? Why aren't there any Hula Hoops or chalk? Why are we caged in with this gate? Why is the ground cement?*

The one thing that poor kids always have in abundance is innovation and imagination. So we filled that lot with screams of joy, "Tag, you're it," and "Goaaalllll" as we kicked bottles into a makeshift goal. The older kids were doing much more mature things, braiding each other's hair, flirting, or bee-bopping. Once in a while, an impromptu dance battle like we watched on *Soul Train* would ensue, with the rest of us either serving as audience members, background dancers, or hopeful backups in case someone got hurt. There was an annual kite day that I remember looking forward to. Mommy bought me a cheap one at a Party City or one of these dollar thrift stores. My class's time, however, was cut short because of my substitute teacher, Mr. Quigley, and his desire to prove a point—which he felt could only be made during kite time. (I always refer to Mr. Quigley as my second grade substitute teacher, but he actually was the only teacher I had in my new school. The regular teacher was there for one day. The only thing I remember was she was white, had glasses, was very timid, appeared scared, and had no control of the class. The next—my second day as a newbie—we were told her daughter was in an accident. She never returned.)

Mr. Quigley at that time seemed like a weird mismatch for the school. First, he was the first male educator I had. Second, he was "white white" as we used to say (the first white to mean his race, the second to emphasize his squareness). Third, he was "white white" in Trenton. He wasn't that old, maybe late thirties or early forties, but he was serious about each of us finishing our work. Which wasn't a problem for me. I would act up a bit because I finished my work super quick and was hella bored in his class. And sometimes he would tell me to step out or send me to another room; I'd cry. But I realized that I enjoyed math problems. I like puzzles, solving them fast, and being distracted from other things I couldn't control. Whenever I got bored, I'd do my homework in class. My curiosity caused me to peek ahead at the next chapter: a new lesson equaled a new challenge, which meant more puzzles! And then I finished the book. When Mr. Quigley said he was going to speak to my father, I got super nervous. The last time my father was contacted by a white person at school, my sister and I were kicked out. And I knew my dad wasn't believing me when my response to "where's your homework?" was "I did it in class." Plus, I didn't want my parents to know about my semi-bratty ways in the classroom.

I have no idea what they talked about, or when they talked, but I do know that eventually, Mr. Quigley gave me more math books, with more problems. He even let me check my answers with his answer key from time to time. I couldn't really appreciate that I was teaching myself up to what would be algebra-level math. The joy of being right and not feeling like I was being punished for being over the daily lessons was enough.

And on kite day, I was really over the daily lesson. Looking outside and seeing all the kids during their scheduled time periods scream as their kites caught the wind and rose was starting to make me sick. *Mr. Quigley and these stupid lessons! We only get one kite day!* His lesson was more like *Jeopardy*: he was waiting for us to guess what the answer to his clue, "a huge space for storing extra items." It's not like we didn't give good guesses. "Basement" and "attic" were the two most repeated answers. Mr. Quigley didn't flinch. Just stared at us, like the only thing that would defrost his cold ass was the right answer. The cries of seven- and eight- (and some nine-) year-olds meant nothing to him. *Like, how many more spaces are there to store extra stuff?* One of my equally annoyed classmates said what I was thinking, *"We don't even have a basement or attic. All we got is a house."* Most of us didn't even have that; we all lived in Section 8 housing, the projects, or multifamily units with a huge emphasis on "multi." But whatever, when your favorite cartoon is *Care Bears*, the place you sleep at is your house.

The cold man turned his head. We held our breath. "It's a kind of house."

HOPE filled the room and a new wave of strong polysyllabic guesses came through. "Tree house!" "Grandma's house!" "Store house!" "Care house!"

Mr. Quigley twirls. "It rhymes with care house!"

So what does my younger self do? I proceed to go through the entire alphabet, starting with *"Bear house! Deer house! Fear house! Gear house!"* I didn't care if it was a real word or not. I just knew we had only 15 minutes until our outside time period was over. I'm damn near out my seat, classmates are going wild as I'm sprinting through the alphabet, and as I get to *"tear house"* I'm having two real thoughts: I know it's not *zeer house* because that sounds silly (although I later learned "zeer" is a thing), but I also know whatever this word is, I've never heard it before. And then, I unlocked the mystery.

"Warehouse!"

A rare, smiling Mr. Quigley throws his hands up. "Kids, go outside."

Jubilee erupted. My desk was covered with erasers, mechanical pencils, candy—whatever my fellow mini-peers had on them. Kids who hadn't spoken to me since I came to the school were now giving congratulatory hugs on their way out. I ran out with my kite, so glad to just see what this pastime was all about. Still unwinding my kite, a real gust came by our cement park. My red and yellow kite danced upward as I was trying to control the direction in what was becoming a me-against-the-wind situation. I attempted to run with my kite, like I saw the other kids doing, but after a short trot, the string got caught in another kite, snapping my rope. As I watched the wind carry the red and yellow cloth, I didn't even have time to cry, although I could feel the tears welling in my chest. I just watched the other kids until it was time to go back inside.

The next day, Mr. Quigley walked me to a room a couple doors down. The room was well-lit and had way fewer kids. I now know it was a gifted and talented class. I assume that was my new classroom for the rest of the year; I don't have any more memories of seeing my classmates or Mr. Quigley.

Sister Fox Is Racist. And I Hate History.

While the feeling of not belonging and being an outsider was not new, the awareness of my poverty was heightened when my sister and I enrolled in an all-girls private school in Princeton. In total there were maybe 20 Black girls in the pre-K—12th grade school of about 400; my sister and I were already two (I don't think she had any other Black girls in her first grade class), there were three other ones in my third-grade class. My cousin Beatrice was in the high school there (and actually was the daughter of the uncle whose address we used to use to go to the better school). We knew one other Black girl in middle school, Roni, who used to claim Bobby Brown's R&B hit was named after her (we definitely believed her). That's almost half the Black girl population.

I immediately hated how I felt in that school, but I also loved the space I was in. And by space, I mean there was so much of it. The school was nestled in a woodsy area, where deer visited salt licks and brooks sang softly against moss and rocks. I thought I had seen playgrounds, but it's different spinning on a merry-go-round, surrounded by trees that touch the sun. Rainy days made us sad, but the teachers made up for it by setting up the library with card games and plenty of art supplies while some classics like *The Sound of Music* were playing (one of my favorite movies to this day). They liked using French terms to describe simply shit; we had *goûter* every day, a fancy way of basically saying "recess with snacks." We had our own lockers (with locks) to change into our gym uniforms. And even though it took an hour and some change to be bussed every day, the destination was worth it. Minus the constant reminder that this world was not created for me.

None of the teachers or girls in the almost all-white, predominantly Catholic school held a sign that screamed, "YOU DON'T BELONG HERE." And honestly, I didn't feel, initially, that I didn't belong. Coming to such a different world at age seven, I probably was thinking, *How do I fit in?* How does a girl like me get these other girls to be my friend? And how do I get these teachers to be as nice to me as they were to the other girls? Aesthetically, I knew I was not their kind of "cute." My nose wasn't pointy, my lips were bigger, my hair was fine in texture but not full, and my face was plagued with plastic beige glasses for my already "imperfect" eyesight. And while we wore uniforms, it's amazing the many ways you can showcase materialism. I didn't have an heirloom passed down from my grandmother or a whole bunch of different-colored slouch socks or scrunchies (those elastic hair accessories, wrapped in fabric, often matching your outfit). Every first day of school, Christmas, or birthday was a dread because it was very evident that I didn't get anything new—or worth noticing. And socially, I wasn't invited to much. I do remember getting birthday invites from girls who barely talked to me, but that probably was because their parents invited the whole class, not because they cared whether their daughter and I actually spoke. After a while, it was evident that I couldn't go to much because I didn't have anyone to drive me there—or back. Both of my parents worked multiple jobs, most times with sharing one car, just to make ends meet, which included the tuition for my sister and me. There was no way I was gonna badger them about Hillary's bat mitzvah.

All humans desire some form of recognition. This is especially true with young people. *I don't have the looks, money, or house like these folks. So what can I DO?* I learned over time that the only way I was going to be somewhat seen—and treated comparably—was through production. I was always a creative child, but if I was gonna draw, I was drawing for the gods, you hear me! If I wrote a poem, I was replicating Shakespearean sonnets. If I was gonna sing, I was gonna sound like Ariel in *The Little Mermaid*. And I loved field day: nothing screamed momentary success like beating all the white girls in the 100-meter dash. I won awards, got some claps, but I hadn't quite cracked the "like me for me" code. And for six years, that really sucked.

What also really sucked was class. My first memory of American History was in fourth grade. The focus of that year was the great exploration of the early "Americans"—which for them were the pilgrims and settlers.

Enter my smart ass, "*Well, if they settled, doesn't that mean wherever they settled already existed?*"

The response was something like, "*Well, they settled after they discovered America?*"

I raised my hand again in confusion, but didn't wait to be called on before I said, "*But how can there be a Thanksgiving if there were people already here? Where did they come from? Did they discover America, too?*"

Annoyed teacher and students alike turned red. I waited, because I was really trying to understand. You see, at this point, I was convinced that I wasn't studious enough in American History and that's why I had a B−/C average in that class. My essay responses, according to my teachers, didn't demonstrate a "grasp" of the "facts" they were sharing in the class. And when you have Nigerian parents who have no room for anything but an A, I wanted to make sure I asked all that I needed to so that I wouldn't be punished for low grades.

At nine, I felt like I was being tortured. I asked questions that made this particularly sister mad. Other kids whispered or rolled their eyes when I raise my hand. And after a while, I stopped participating because I noticed other patterns that led me to a conclusion that I shared out loud one day: Sister Fox is racist.

"*Excuse me, young lady?*"

I calmly repeated it. "*Sister Fox is racist.*"

If you were to ask me then all the things that made that statement true, it would have been difficult. Whether it was that I had to ask repeatedly to use the bathroom, was overly scrutinized for my penmanship (my cursive was beautiful), or her inability to say nice things to me, about me, the way she did other kids. And also—that hunch. The hunch of "when you know, you know"—even though white spaces force you to articulate a feeling without words. Or at least believable words. My words weren't believable though. I could tell once I said it—and then repeated it—that I was in trouble.

I know my parents were called, and only through my parents was I made aware that they had said something to the effect that the school wanted me to speak to some type of counselor about these "feelings." My parents hadn't told me what to expect—they may not have even known. But they didn't scold me for my conclusion that Sister Fox was racist. They asked me why I felt that way, and I presented my argument that it wasn't a feeling, and that based on the definition of *racist*, that she and others were showing prejudice toward me and others who looked like me. In hindsight, I didn't feel like I was speaking with my parents like I was a child; we were gathered as a mini-council.

Nevertheless, it didn't seem like I had a choice as to whether or not I would meet this counselor. The first time I met this person, I was shocked because he was a man (which is jarring in an all-girls school). He described himself as a psychologist and said things like "We want to help you with why you are upset and angry." I didn't respond. On that first visit, I recall there being some markers and paper in the room, so I went over and just started drawing. What sucked was that I had these sessions during my beloved *goûter*, while my classmates were outside with nature, I was in here with this white man asking me questions about my life and none about Sister Fox.

Do your parents beat you?

I stopped coloring, but I didn't look up. At that moment, I felt like a totally different experience was occurring. It was clear we weren't there to explore why I was othered, or me being lonely the majority of the day. I also knew that this was about something beyond me: fault, blame, punishment. But not of Sister Fox. Of my family, my parents. Poor working immigrants who somewhat trusted this process, partially because they were somewhat blind to socialized racism themselves; it's always been difficult to fully engage them on this topic. Their connection to the harms of white spaces was limited as they were raised in villages where everyone looks just like you and all protect children. That question made me feel ashamed—of what, I didn't know. I just knew I no longer wanted to participate. So I just answered him.

"*No.*"

I would later be approached by one of the few older Black girls in the school, Najée, who told me she heard about what happened and that the same thing happened to her. She advised me, *Be pleasant and cordial in those sessions. Don't say too much in there. They're not gonna believe you anyway. They'll make it seem like it's all your fault and blame you. And they're gonna think you're crazy.* I took every word like it was a roadmap. Before I was 10 years old, I had my first conscious lesson about how to survive in white-dominant spaces, how to code switch, and what not to expect from them.

From that day, I always knew that when someone said "they" it meant white folks. It was around that time that I also got validation that, yes, others with my complexion and features also were treated differently. The only thing that made it so hard was that I was 10. Was my whole life going to be like this?

Two Poor Girls Walk into a Dorm in West Virginia . . .

Living in West Virginia taught me a lot about . . . life. My freshman roommate, Rachel, and I were both full scholarship recipients at WVU. We lived in the corner of the honors dorm—which actually was reserved for three students, but our third roommate never moved in. I moved in a couple days before Rachel, making the long drive with my parents and a couple of my siblings from Trenton, New Jersey, all the way to West Virginia. I'll never forget that day—it was a Saturday. When my family drove off, I stared at this empty room that only had desks and bunk beds. *Are we supposed to furnish this room? With what? With what money?* Not even up to an hour until my parents drove off, I started to get hungry. And then I froze: I had no money. I didn't own a cellphone yet, but everything in me wanted to let my family know that we'd forgotten about food. I quickly realized that "full scholarship" is not the same as "all inclusive." And with the dorm cafeterias not even open yet for the school term, my seventeen-year-old self felt the fullness of my poverty right at that moment.

My fast broke the next day when my roommate arrived with her family. When I first met her, I was nervous: she was nice, sweet, but also seemed scared of me, as did her entire family. Little did she know I was scared of her, too. I didn't really grow up trusting white people, and with the exception of a few sleepovers, culture shock was setting in that we would be cohabitating. Knowing what I know now about bias, I can only imagine what was going on through her head. But after speaking with each other, we realized we had a bit in common: we both were scholarship recipients, the oldest out of five children, Christian, and poor. Hmm, well that's where the similarities ended. But when she offered me a sandwich, I realized that while neither one of us would trade our experiences for the others, that didn't mean we weren't capable of seeing parts of each other.

Rachel's first year seemed really enjoyable; she received a lot of support from the residential campus and recognition for being an honors scholar. I didn't receive the same kind of treatment. I studied hard and was doing well, but over time, I recognized that the environment was not supportive of Black students at all. In addition to low representation, if you weren't a male athlete on the football or basketball team, you kind of had to find your own way. And eventually, I found a crew I vibed with. But the blatant and subtle racial aggressions—from administrators to students—coupled with the white fraternity energy, drinking, and reports of rampant sexual assaults—made me anxious about my safety almost all the time. The few times I discussed this with my roommate, I realized that while she was a good listener, she couldn't relate. Her focus was to be on top so she could overcome poverty. I had the same goal, except I had to maneuver the intersection of being Black, a woman, and surrounded by a very white culture.

Humans have the ability to make memorable, positive moments in any environment, even oppressive ones. And I had some great moments at college. But for both my undergraduate and graduate studies, I struggled, and I think eventually just surrendered. I no longer had expectations of being seen by white peers. I lost faith in any system intended to support survivors of sexual assault. And despite my academic achievements, I was second-guessed by professors often, many of whom challenged my intelligence or "mansplained" concepts I already knew. I realized I couldn't rely on this particular institution to support my career journey and became more and more self-sufficient and independent—which for the longest time I prided myself on, but today I recognize the fatigue and exhaustion of that reality. I was thrilled to leave West Virginia. Little did I know that it was merely preparing me for the reality that every space was the same.

When I discuss white-dominant cultures, I like to lead with examples (and there are so many) of how normal it is. There is no door called "white-dominant culture"; we're born into it. And to be clear, white-dominant culture wasn't working for my roommate's family either. Yes, they were white, but they were economically disenfranchised. Her degree was literally the baton to help advance her entire family. But even though she could see our economic similarities, what I was experiencing as a Black young woman was inaccessible to her. And while she tried to offer advice as a means of support, all of her offerings were about me adjusting to systems, not about my environment changing for people like me. Because to discuss changing the system would also mean changing her access to a new level of power. She never questioned our environment, which by default meant that she either did not see how unfair my experience was, or she blamed me for my experiences. This, too, is a byproduct of white-dominant culture.

We Just Want Clean Water

Detroit and its surrounding area has held a special place in my heart since my first visit there in 2004 as a law student. There were so many similarities between the once-industrial pillar of our nation and my hometown of Trenton. The chipped bricks of now abandoned multi-family homes, factories, and stores bore the tale of bitter divorce between the American Dream and American workers. Every day, families pay the hefty debt of navigating segregation, food apartheid, and inadequate public transportation to perform basic functions to survive. Like in my hood, the hard-working people of Motor City embody James Baldwin's quote, "Anyone who has ever struggled with poverty knows how extremely expensive it is to be poor." Being on the ground during the Flint water crisis made this very real for me.

I actually had been on the ground prior to the water contamination scandal, working with activists to address so many civil and human rights concerns. The activists were a cross-section of community leaders—young people, voting experts, clergy, and seasoned retirees. I had seen them in action before. So when I was asked to come back to help make the water crisis an election issue, I was more than happy to go. But when I got on the ground, it was mostly the same people, but they weren't the same. The impact of fighting for water was all over their faces. When I went to hug one of the nuns, she cautioned me with, "Not on the left side, dear." I could see there was a growth on her neck.

When I pulled up the first slide of my training, I asked the room, "What would it look like if all the needs of Detroit were met?" The usually boisterous group stared at me as if the question was just so far off base. And at that moment, it may have been.

"Ify, I can't think about if we'll ever matter," one of the younger activists said. "We just want clean water."

(Personal) #CultureChat

To be a designer in this work requires one to have tools and materials. One of those materials is your personal journey through this work. Whether you recognized in the moment or are reflecting on moments in hindsight, we all have encountered equity moments in our lives. The stories I've just shared reveal both how I was making sense of a white-dominant culture, as well as observing how the standards and norms were impacting others around me. As you do this work, having a healthy relationship with your journey is vital. Lived experiences give us an opportunity to ask the following questions:

- What do I wish I knew when I was younger?
- How would I have responded differently if I were in that situation again?
- In what ways did I wish the world responded to me or others differently?

It is hard for movements to be sustainable without a deep connection to their success. Think of three moments over the span of your life that you believe helped shape your awareness of equity and answer those three questions. Once you're done reflecting, how do those moments inform the way you desire to shift cultures today? Jot that down and keep it close.

Designing New Journeys with an Equity Mindset

By Nik Walker (he/him), Actor and Writer

The pandemic seemed to provide a space, and a time, and a pause, in the midst of death, and uprising to truly reevaluate how we do things. And it was very clear that so many promises were made during that rest time, and then when we returned to work (theater), we wondered if those promises would be upheld. And I think we very quickly saw the places where promises were not upheld, and those places grew on their own, like cavities in a tooth. It was almost like we tried to "capitalism" our way out of the pandemic. So then once we got out of the shutdown phase, not only are we trying to find equity post shutdown, but we are also having to dig ourselves out of the hole we dug ourselves in, because we tried to capitalism our way out of a pandemic. So, it's a war on several fronts, and people, at the end of the day, want their money back. Right? And what's crazy about the arts is that at the very crux of what we do is this idea of how can we share stories with people? Empathy. That's what we try to do is create empathy, but we are at the intersection of art and commerce. So it's creating empathy and making a buck for it. So what is the bare minimum that needs to be done to create empathy and make a buck on it? And not that everyone's going with that mindset, but I think that that mindset's pull is so strong that what you find are people who aren't ready to have the conversation. They aren't ready to really do the work and understand what it is that reflection actually is. Because it's not just "do this and it will be fine"; instead it's "do this and start a journey that redefines your entire life and your way of working." And so are you really ready to come with us on this

(Continued)

journey? And I think that what I have found in my year and a half back to Broadway, is that while I think everyone's hearts are in the right place, or most people's hearts are in the right place, there is often an underestimation of the wall that is capitalism; the wall that is produced and run roughshod over people's need to be heard and treated equitably. If you view it as digging your way out of a hole, then you're focused on the digging . . . you're not focused on the people who are helping you dig. And I think that that's often where we find ourselves, especially now in the arts because, you know, so many things are changing so rapidly, it just feels like we often don't take time, because we don't feel we have time, because we don't understand our place in this culture anymore.

What gives me hope, in the thing, is understanding that the best way to beat capitalism, in my personal opinion, is to remove our belief in the value of the things that capitalism finds valuable. Your work doesn't have to be on the biggest screen. It doesn't have to be on the big streaming platform. It doesn't have to be on the biggest stage. Right? But can you gather a group of people? And can you have them come see your thing? Or come read your thing? Or come work on your thing? And can you find a way to pay them a good wage? Those basics of the thing, if that's the mindset you go into your project with, then all the rest of it you understand as like, "extra." I think that's when we get in trouble: when we look at the extra as the thing right now. The fact that a product does well and sells and people want a franchise, that's actually extra. That's not the "thing." The thing, the community, the art the community created together, that is the thing.

So yes, that might take longer. No, that might not hit in the way that your mom, and dad wanted it to hit. But did you do it in a way that was true to your vision that respected everybody that came on board with you? These are the things that I think we have to just engage with more and take more value in the uncertainty of trying to understand. And that may mean that certain rooms aren't for you. And that may mean that you are truly making a choice to say, "At this moment, I value my happiness and the equity of my friends and the people I work with on these things more than a check." And I will understand that by doing this I might be signing up for a little less money.

#EquityMindset with Javier Lopez

Javier Lopez (he/him) is a social-impact strategist who specializes in transforming communities by centering credible messengers with culturally relevant lived experiences. He has also advised public health spaces on how to transfer the intelligence of violence interrupters into pandemic support and outreach networks.

Ify: Hey, Javi! How are you?

Javi: Everything is good. I can say that with confidence. Everything is good. Professionally, in a good place. Kids are here. You know, I teach every now and then too. I love it. Kids are living, they're healthy. They're active all over the place. And my wife and I have good energy, good relationship. So like everything is . . .

Ify: Copacetic!

Javi: Yo, and I used to front on sharing that like, "Yo, everything is good." Because sometimes, you know how it goes when the share-outs happen: people be going through it.

	But I got to lift up the good things because somebody's giving me these gifts. You know.
Ify:	I think that's the perfect way to even start this conversation, especially amongst equity practitioners. I want to talk about your journey and also joy. But I want to start with the joy part because you just raised it. Can you share why joy is important to sustain a real equity movement? If I can be completely honest, there are moments where even though organizations speak as if they want our presence, I still feel a real resistance to just being our full selves and being joyful. And actually getting comfortable. And as soon as we get a little too comfortable, or it's too many of us within an organization, then the efforts stop. Like everything gets taken away. So can you talk about the power of joy and why it's needed? And maybe a little bit about why there is such a resistance to us experiencing joy in spaces?
Javi:	God, that's a good question. So I think the resistance is rooted in a subculture of perpetually being in "the struggle" all the time that says that there's some validation to your legitimacy when you're forever fighting. And it's gone mainstream into how people are viewing the work that we do. In many ways, we've been conditioned to lead with, "We went through so much and this process is so hard and dealing with all these white folks is so daunting and trying to gain equity and justice is forever, and we're pushing this boulder up a hill." And that's all true, right? And, also, in each of those moments, successes happen while you're pushing that boulder up. But, sometimes, we feel we can't celebrate too much, because it might stifle progress, or what we got is not everything. And I just think that we've been given the wrong guidance of how to view the journey. Like, I think we've been given the guidance that the journey is always this hard thing, that if

you don't get everything that you're fighting for—personally and professionally—you can never be happy. Personally, I just decided that my success is going to be rooted in what's going on in my life. My happiness and my joy is gonna be rooted in my kids and my wife and how my relationship with them is, and that's going to influence how I relate to the work. So I need to be joyful. I need to be happy, you know. To get the best out of my work.

What I give to people, you know, when I'm not happy? Man, I think that used to show up frequently. So when I would focus only on that boulder up the hill, and all the hard work being stressful, my personal life wasn't on point. And that was a duality of stressors that I didn't get right. And I don't think I was the best practitioner, best worker, or best person. So joy gives me personal satisfaction. Like, I can vibe with my wife—that's a big deal. We've been together for 17 years, first as girlfriend/boyfriend, and now as husband and wife, right? And then my kids, they're smiling, they're happy, they're physically able to move around. All that joy sits in me. So then when I'm doing work on changing the Cross Bronx Expressway, which is a project I'm on, or getting more communities of color in the Special Olympics of New York, from an equity and justice standpoint that's all daunting, that's all hard, and I'm dealing with people that don't understand what I'm talking about all the time. But you're not going to take away my joy. You may stress me, but you're not going to take away my joy. So I think we need to go back to recognizing that we can be joyful in the struggle.

Ify: And we need the space to be joyful, right, even at work. Many organizational spaces have good intentions with creating identity spaces, like through these employee resource groups, where people with shared experiences can come together. And those spaces are needed. But our joy should not be limited to those spaces. And part of this codesign is creating practices with people from diverse identities and experiences to just "be." There's an opportunity we miss when communities don't come together. And I'm working on this, too. Showing up with my whole humaneness, which includes my real jokes and also some of my real hardships, if the safety is there. It's definitely a mindset thing, fam. Like, I think this whole equity journey for me: holding space for joy in the midst of spaces that aren't used to my being is a mental leap at times. The way I'm wired, I can be laser focused on making sure leaders know the culture we inherited and how to create new systems. It's like we don't even get to the joy part because the focus is correcting history and data. But simultaneously there's this growth part that I think you're introducing, which includes dropping some of that—whatever it means to be perfect in our movements, or feeling that we have to portray how we're fighting for liberation in a certain way. It's about identifying where the safety is for us to show all the facets of what it takes to actually push against that boulder. And I needed that reminder on the fuel of joy, which sometimes gets missed in conversation. And it's not just us. Even for people that are trying to be allies or in solidarity. Understandably, they lean full force into this hardship, maybe in response to what they perceive is our struggle. I've definitely held space for those struggling with the guilt of their privilege. And, yes, when in our spaces especially, they should be responsible, be accountable, be aware. And also know that when you're coming to me, we may also be cracking some jokes even in moments of conflict or tension. Which is also why I think people love our culture; in spite of what we've gone through, we still show joy. The things that should have killed us didn't. It doesn't diminish the struggle. But it does mean we're still out here.

Javi: Listen, we're still gonna play the congas, we're still gonna go out dancing. Like, as a cis person that has been in many different gender-identity spaces with different intersectionalities—I don't do this anymore—but I used to just sit back and be quiet. Like, I didn't say anything, because I felt that all the privilege that I have as a cis man in these spaces, and all this privilege I have in this world, I couldn't really talk about how those privileges gave me joy, right? How those privileges have extended me a smile and allow me to experience life differently—while also acknowledging everything that's happening around me. And then one day, I just decided, like, I'm gonna share who I am, you know what I mean. I'm gonna share my full self, like, "Yo, I was able to be able-bodied and participate in this marathon in the male category. And it gave me great joy because I met a personal mark and yadda, yadda," right—just like that, all in that space. And I was received, and it felt great, just being myself. And honestly, I just started to understand even more deeply the responsibility I had to all of us in that community. Like you said, there's a level of being fixed and clear on what we're ultimately here to do and understanding and respecting the many lived experiences and struggles in the room. But, yo, if you can't be celebratory, if you can't be happy, if you can't share that with people, then you're doing a disservice to the movement.

Ify: I'm about to switch it up on us a bit, and that is the baseline of whiteness as the bar. We've all been conditioned to see that as the measure to compare well-being and wellness up against. And I struggle with that because I do think it distracts from the actual goals, including being free from barriers. And I desire that for all people.

Javi: Yea, this happened in public health work all the time when I was in that space—always a comparison to white communities. And I was like, "that's not the bar." That's not the goal. The goal was for us to have access to what privileged communities had access to, but even deeper than that: to write our own chapters. Our chapters—whatever that looks like—is not about them, you know? It's completely unwritten. It's not fully here yet, right? It's to be determined by us, for us. That's our bar.

But let me also say something about privilege. I always share who I am: a cishet Puerto Rican man. And putting that out there is very much needed. Why? Because I want people to ask me, *What are you getting? What are you experiencing?* I want them to know what my privileges afford me because that's what they deserve as well. We can be each other's baseline, even if we don't have maximum privilege. I just did this with somebody the other day, a Dominican brother who was helping out my son with baseball, and I was like, "Yo, bro, like, you should get your LLC going." He shared that he was an immigrant from the DR and that he doesn't know anything outside of what he's been doing for baseball over the last 15 years. But I got all this privilege. I got all this access. I'm bilin-gual. I got all these things. So I'm putting them on to game, and I think that just that element of being able to share, from an equity standpoint, a growth mindset, that has to be something that we regularly practice. And create community systems that enable that care.

Ify: I love that example, because so many times when we talk about equity, people think we're talking at people, instead of connecting with people and problem solving together. Even within marginalized communities and our shared struggles, centering each other's deservingness is key. When I think of how we do that optimally, there's an unlearning that must happen first. Yes, we belong to marginalized communities, and we have also learned how to internally harm as well as harm those within our communities. And it's hurting us. Anti-blackness is global. Anti-trans, even within queer spaces, is global. Ableism is global. And now more than ever we need to be connected with each other. But, in addition to surviving, I do think there are some community introspective chats which are overdue, including anti-blackness within immigrant spaces. And that includes Caribbean and African immigrants as well.

Javi: Unlearning is essential. There's a certain tonality with how we, in movement, work and lead discussions that are presented as absolutes. I think about the ways in which we discuss anti-blackness or intersectionality or gender identity, and there's an absolute type of tone, like you could only talk about it this way, or you can only have a discussion in this manner. And it's complicated, right? We have people who provide safeguards in a space to protect against more harm. No one likes any form of harm coming their way either. But my observation is that in the discussion of these matters and in leading this work, we have prevented our own growth. I think we have to have more room for people to fuck up more when we're in community. We've become too perfect that those who need support unlearning aren't anywhere near the room. And the world doesn't give us that grace to make mistakes.

Sometimes we have to remember that humans are mistake-prone; we have to give our people space to make mistakes. We also have to allow more room for the conversation, man. Like we just have abandoned conversation. We've even abandoned conversation within ourselves. Everybody's always trying to one-up each other from a standpoint, like, who's got "the most" in this work? Like, who can speak out the best? Who can show out the best? Who can get the applause? Who can get the snaps? We have to unlearn all that because there's no best because we're all still struggling. So like, if we're still struggling, we have to reflect on how we're doing it and how we're showing up. And I think we're doing it in a manner that's rooted in pure academia without the grace our communities beautifully hold. I think we have to let go of that validation of presenting things in that matter. Because that's not, that's not giving us anything, but maybe giving us some speaking engagements. So I think this academic framing, and how we present professionalism, and the lack of room and space for that cousin or auntie who honestly don't got it yet, we gotta give them the space to mess up and correct with love.

Ify: Safety is absolutely important. But if we're gonna invite people into alternative ways of orienting with the world which they were socialized to accept as normal, academia is the least community way of doing that. And by creating no way for community members to enter, we may actually be leaving out some of the people who may actually be the designers we need, if not now, in the future. Yes, even the ones who've harmed, right? That means Abuela, who grew up treating her grandchildren a certain way based on complexion. Even Abuela deserves a conversation. And we must also believe that Abuela is a part of the solution, that she has some wisdom around care and protection. She can evolve in how she views humanity and what her role is in this equity movement. And I think that that's actually the harder part about equity and transformative justice—seeing those who harm as also potential designers of our interconnected fate.

Javi: And people are awakening all the time. They don't believe in all the stuff they've been taught, but they are struggling to really articulate their concerns. For example, different gender-identity norms are just coming into some of our spaces and consciousness. I know this man who was struggling with that, but he didn't want to say it. He really doesn't know what to say and doesn't want to offend. But if we're having a true conversation, right, and I give him space to express himself, and what follows is "I don't believe in X, Y, and Z," and I'm a person of color that lives in his community—I may not agree with all of his stuff. But do we want to shun him and be like, "Boo, boo, get out"? I'm gonna be like, "Yo, we got to talk about that. What is it about that's giving you pause? Because you got great ideas about other things that we also need your wisdom on." We really have to abandon the doctrine of perfectionism and be receptive to talking to people as long as they ain't trying to hurt you. Once we're on the same page that you wouldn't want to hurt me and that you ain't trying to hurt the people we're talking about, then we can talk. And we may need to talk again. And then let's build. Let's build on this. And I learned a lot of that, through the credible-messenger-related work, where you're meeting people in a very imperfect manner. Real talk, you can't expect someone to come at you and meet you in a certain respectable way, when they have all these adverse experiences, including being tangled in these legal systems. It's not about excuses; it's about understanding. There are so many thought processes competing—what they want to do, how they want to live their life—that they're still working through. You can't expect all of them to be ready to go with whatever the ideal is.

Ify: About to make a quick pivot. You just mentioned the credible-messenger piece, which has me thinking about this larger "proximity" conversation: those who are the most proximate to the harm are supposed to be closest to the solutions. My question is, where's the room for solution-making? Because I'm still not seeing enough of those who are the most proximate in positions of power and leadership.

Javi: That's because no one wants to say what we're really experiencing: power doing what power does. The real deal is when you're starting a business, the ones closest to the business run the business. Like you don't usually say, "You know what, we're going to let someone make that determination of how my restaurant is going to be set up, or how my company is going to be set up" right? Dominant culture doesn't see "those closest to the solution" as sharing power. It has been whitewashed as a concept, and the power of it has been minimized.

Ify: I've similarly been struggling with the overuse of the term "lived experiences." We are missing the power of its potency when we see it as a garnish versus an actual ingredient in the recipe. And what I'm observing is fatigue and retraumatizing when the sharing of one's experience doesn't yield much fruit. Marginalized voices should not only be brought in during months where themed diversity is celebrated. Naw, solidarity moves differently. It's almost like lived experiences and credible messages are only in our spaces when we want it, but maybe not seeing the maximum power of those experiences, or in our solidarity. And part of that is that some folks haven't imagined what it is like to actually make space for those most impacted to lead. It starts with a vision first.

Javi: And with ownership, right? In the business world, equity is ownership of something. It's like a commodity, you own something. We got to own our experiences, which includes how we invest time, space, and energy. I totally think that the whole reclaiming of language, the whole reclaiming of what it means when we say "equity," is a step toward a revolution. Otherwise, we're compounding the trauma by allowing the language to be manipulated and codified and put out there in ways counter to the truth. It really is up to us to stop that. Further, we need to invest in each other with cooperative investment strategies. And we need space to figure this out.

Ify: Mm hmm. Thank you, Javier.

12 | Centering Proximate Leadership in Our Research Practices

Riddle me this: With all these research-led advocacy groups, why haven't we solved more problems?

Research has always been a space reserved for the elite, educated, and accredited. And in some ways, it's a hustle. To be tenured at most universities, for example, an educator must produce a certain number of peer-reviewed articles. The art of being published is, in itself, a game. Dr. Monnica T. Williams's article, "Racism in Academic Publishing," reveals how being top-tier in the world of research means creating content that can get published, that is, catering to the mostly white-dominated audience:

> ... my success as a research psychologist hinges on my ability to keep churning out high-quality, publishable, scientific material—an endeavor made doubly difficult because most of my scholarship is about race, racism, and mental health inequities. I have found that

these are not favored topics by editors and reviewers, and it can be easier for them to *desk reject* an article than do the work of identifying qualified people for peer review.[1]

Of course, no one tells you in third grade that the majority of research stems from such an exclusive and competitive space that lacks diversity and curiosity. The long pipeline of education, formal and informal, tells us to trust scientific approaches and outcomes. And embedded in that socialization is the soft whisper of "they know more than you do."

I personally remember this pressure in graduate school. After spending much of undergrad not being clear on what I wanted to do with my life, I got accepted into my school's applied communication studies master's program. At the time, I was interested in leveraging the research and statistics practices I'd learned to find out more about my people; specifically our behaviors and communication styles in white-dominant spaces and how we maneuvered health and organizational communications. But I found much of the existing research just "off"; body language interpretations, for example, like crossing one's arms, being seen as automatically aggressive was news to me—especially since it was one of my default stances. *Is this partially why I'm asked, "Is everything okay?" so many times by them?* I wondered.

While I was interested in learning how we responded to white spaces, the one-year intensive course was laser focused on one thing: peer-reviewed articles. And with an almost entirely white male faculty, I found it hard to find guidance and mentorship into a possible PhD in what I was calling "urban communication" (I would never call it this today, by the way). The best advice I received was to apply to another school, design the program I was seeking to graduate in, and then enroll in it. At 22, that felt too daunting. And while I had managed to be a researcher on a couple published articles and to present at conferences, I knew I didn't belong in that space. My ego wasn't aligned with where the majority of the field was: competition and bragging rights. I didn't care about that. I cared about exploring how we maneuvered day-to-day living and how people who grew up like me made decisions about life.

Upon reflection, I think I was also trying to figure out why I didn't fit in; being in a very homogenous state like West Virginia had me feeling like I was in a Petri dish every day. After enduring long nights running stats, weekly exams, and several drafts of research I didn't care about, I graduated as the second Black woman from that program (my sorority sister was the first, graduating the year prior). But that experience had a chilling effect on me: most researchers have other competing interests attached to their work and they are not proximate to the phenomena they are researching, nor do their personal lives rely on the research for their survival. *If we're only researching what will get published, and we only see what gets published, how will we see the work that matters to the majority? And when will they be at the center of the work, not just the subjects?*

If we believe those closest to the harm are the ones closest to the solution, then we need to abandon our traditional ways of viewing research and engage in more disruptive ways of being.

Testing Current Assumptions about "Community-Led" Mindsets

While several institutions are using community and partnership language, there is this false belief that providing space for marginalized communities to share and providing resources to communities is enough. The reality is that too many of the mission-centered organizations that receive funding to study our communities under a microscope lack proximate knowledge of how oppression has shaped attitudes, survival skills, and necessary innovations. Institutions employing an equity mindset have the power to shift how those least proximate to power are perceived by using language that demonstrates their leadership, and backing that language by creating meaningful spaces for contributions to be shared and implemented.

To do that, however, organizations must challenge the following assumptions:

- Remove the concept of "charity" from your institutions' psyche. Communities are not waking up in the morning waiting for you to save them. Instead, align your equity mission to be about co-development of solutions with those most impacted, and see resources and investments as necessary tools to advance the work.
- Peer-review is not the full story, and may be severely disconnected from the truth. Supplement existing research advisories and reports with insights from researchers who are also members of the community you are centering.
- Recognize that much of existing data blames the communities for what they're experiencing—whether in the framing of the research question, the implementation of fact-gathering techniques, or the analysis. If research focused on the conditions of marginalized communities fails to center the design of systemic racism, that's a flag.
- Engage with communities only if you truly see them as collaborators and co-strategists. This means that many institutions must switch their community-led frameworks from being one of extraction toward being one of shared power.

Respecting Impacted Persons as Innovators and Researchers

During the height of the COVID-19 pandemic, my team served as equity advisors to several institutions that were struggling with communities, partnering with them to co-design solutions. For example, in one community of practice we were facilitating, the question as to why Black communities were lagging in vaccination uptake resulted in the expected deep dive into the well-earned distrust of government and science institutions. But we also raised a missed opportunity. Even as we discuss vaccinations, most leaders aren't even centering helpful historical facts to deepen relationships with oppressed communities. The development of vaccines in the United States actually stems from the wisdom of an enslaved African, Onesimus, whose description of the African and Asian practice of variolation contributed to the development of a response to the smallpox epidemic in the 1700s.

Why is that not taught?

Why are we not connecting the communities that are most harmed with the genius and innovations of their ancestors?

In the spirit of Onesimus, community groups who were a part of this community of practice were not looking to researchers and funders for ideas on how to connect with their neighbors. They possessed a deep understanding of policy, both what it claims it's supposed to do and its actual impact on communities. Their stories are also data; their solutions are data-informed; and their evaluations include a factor that white-dominant institutions don't factor in—trust.

The Power of Community Conversations as a Research Tool

Organizations seeking to meet the needs of those most proximate to the harms of systemic oppression need more impacted parties participating in their work—from problem identification to program design. I'm a huge fan of community conversations, when done right. When there's trust, dialogues reveal more than responses to targeted questions. Dialogues enable folks sharing the same culture to connect with other community members. Dialogues support collaborative solutions among folks who already are designing strategies on a daily basis. And dialogues inform priorities—something that is usually determined by institutions before they engage with communities. If an organization is truly invested in meeting their impact goals, those goals would be created with communities leading the way. Here's a quick guide to maximize the implementation of community conversations:

Pre-work
- Research the communities you seek to engage.
- Identify starting community partners to support the framing of conversations and the right partners to engage with for the conversation.
- Identify a facilitator who understands the community and their experiences.
- Allocate resources to compensate for participation.
- If possible, share ahead of time possible topics that will be explored.

During the conversation
- Center the community, and decenter traditional ways of doing research.
- Acknowledge their history and understand why they matter (this is different than why they are a "priority").
- Acknowledge the time they are giving.
- Acknowledge the labor of this work.
- Acknowledge that they know enough to provide solutions because they've been solving these issues without equitable interventions for decades and generations.
- Decenter the "research" language and broaden toward a dialogue, which invites more perspectives and ensures folks have entry points into the conversation (we are here to measure, examine, assess).
- Listen to lived experiences that explain the impact of policies; be open to narratives with compounded policy issues, as proximate researchers do not live single-issue lives.
- Invite communities to brainstorm policy ideas to advocate on.

After the conversation

- Pay contributors.
- Circle back and confirm and affirm their contributions.
- Share "what's next," including how their insights will be used.

Ongoing

- Advocate for the voice you heard, not the one you wanted to hear (when facing resistance).
- Don't try to make their issues fit with your agenda.
- Explore the other relationships that make it hard to support community voices (funders/internal politics/gatekeepers).
- Don't only engage proximate voices to examine the issues you think they are connected to; lean into a spirit of partnership and mutuality, and find ways to invite them into other aspects that are material and important to your organization.
- Invite contributors to share what would make these conversations more authentic, and don't get offended by their response.

#EquityMindset with Alisha L. Gordon

Alisha L. Gordon (she/hers) is the founder and executive director of *The Current Project*, a nonprofit organization committed to closing the social and economic gaps for Black single mothers. Gordon taps policy and programming initiatives to innovate around social barriers to create pathways for Black mothers.

Ify: Equity is not a solopreneur venture; it is very much one that requires practitioners to be in intentional spaces of learning from other people who are in other spaces, who've mastered maneuvering the burdens of what they've inherited. With your range of leadership that focuses on not just the labor of mothers and women, but the innovations of mothers and women, I want to get your thoughts on why equity is so important in the labor space. What should the mindset be for decision makers who are essential to creating those spaces where women can innovate, where women can thrive? Or even the tools and the practices that need to be learned or unlearned? What needs to be deconstructed?

Alisha: So, a couple of things come to mind, and I can only speak from my social location as a Black femme mother from the South, went from welfare to six figures, and the entire range of those experiences. There's something innate about the social location of Black women, Black mothers, femme women, femme mothers, by sheer social location that calls for innovation—and the calling for innovation around social, economic, political barriers. We've been doing this since the beginning of time. And what has happened in the last millennia is that we've taken the innate . . . we've taken our social locations and the native ability to innovate around barriers, and literally picked them up and put them inside of organizational systems that do not generally have the pathways—and I think that's a really important word—the pathways to nurture the innovation, to ground the innovation, to resource innovation, and to help the innovator get to expand her ability to go wherever it is that she wants to go. And, obviously, this is capitalism, by design. And it's also not lost on me that the unsaid part of the equity mindset is also having the ability to recognize the kinds of stories and traumas that Black mothers and Black femme and Black women, in particular, carry because we've had to learn how to innovate around that, too, in order to show up in these spaces.

An equity mindset is really about—and it's almost an ancestral notion—creating pathways for people; pathways that allow for these kinds of diverging paths. Because taking all this innovation and dumping it into a system that is not designed for people to have multiple paths will have us hitting roadblocks.

Ify: Here is something I don't want to lose, but I think we've almost lost. I was watching a clip around the practice of midwifery in America and the rightful credit to Black women in the South, who preserved from Africa, through the transatlantic slave endeavor, to plantations where the birthing of white babies and Black babies were a priority for two completely different reasons. The birth rates were better than what we have today, in no small part to these Black medical experts. But the system transformed to one of "meritocracy," created by white men to ultimately "grade" who is qualified and who isn't qualified to be a midwife. It changed everything so drastically—to the extent that it erased an entire medical institution of Black femme practitioners, who were replaced by white women. The system created an accreditation to discredit the genius Black women built and sustained. And not because there was a medical reason. Today, we suffer the highest maternal and infant mortality rates.

To your point, it is also bringing a notion of humanity, dignity, and care that is an innovation of who Black people inherently are. We know this to be true because the system of enslavement and everything which stems from that—which is America—was not made for, designed for us to matter and treat each other as if we mattered. That comes from outside the system. So, that "mattering," and I love this "pathway to innovation" you speak of, means that on the other side of you mattering you open yourself up to whatever creativity comes your way.

So, when I think about organizational work, I am now questioning how many people came into organizations thinking that what they saw was "care," but it didn't actually give them the space to thrive. Because, as you are reminding us, the design was never intended to abandon the original design for this innovation of radical self-care. We tend to miss that and not give ourselves credit for that: that the care we experience in organizations is shaped by those most oppressed.

Alisha: I think about my Current Project and the intentional pathways language that we use, and when I say it's ancestral, it takes my mind to the Underground Railroad. It takes my mind to all the places we were travailing and traversing, trying to get to freedom, proverbial or not. And the kind of level of care required to help people get there. It is an ushering of souls of human beings, of human capacity, that helps people get to where they feel they are called to be. And that is often the rub, right? When you talk about organizations, obviously there is a primary goal in mind for that organization, but that goal cannot trump human capacity to thrive. And people who are working within organizations have to have a pathway to have a multifaceted life; to have a life where they are putting efforts and energy into the organization and the organization, in turn, creates the conditions for them to find a pathway by which they are able to express the fullness of what they have the capacity to do. That the work is not just about building up the bottom line of the organization or meeting a sales quota, but is really about

creating conditions where people who bring their inno-
vative and creative ideas into the space to help move the
organization's agenda forward are provided the tools and
space to move their own agenda forward, which often
looks like equitable pay and time off and paternal and
maternal pay.

And it's not just about creating a space to thrive, but
also sustaining the thriving, which means being able to
maintain the level of care—economic, social, and spiritual
well-being—and have it in such abundance that you are
able to put some away for a rainy day. Thriving is not
about hoping you can pay the bills every month. Thriving
is about paying those bills, putting some away for a rainy
day, and being able to sow seed back into the community
because that means you're in a place of abundance.

Ify: And you were making the connection that even if organizations were to put their best foot forward, there are
always these systemic, both explicit and hidden, barriers
that continue to remind us, especially Black women, that
you are actually not intended to thrive and your thriving
is not something that this nation has ever envisioned as
being real and actualized and definitely not in mass, not
for it to be the norm.

Alisha: Right. And then we put certain people up on a pedestal
and say, "Look, she made it, Oprah made it!" But she's
one in a million, right? The real tracking of thriving for
Black women, Black femme folks is when Leticia makes
it and there are 900 just like her that have made it, too.
The thriving of the "least of these" creates a condition for
thriving for everybody. When I imagine a world where
the average everyday person has the capacity not only to
do for themselves but for the community as well because

they are living in abundance, that's the shit dreams are made of! That's the world we should be striving for.

And maybe part of the challenge that organizations experience is trying to understand the importance of this. But I can tell you that having a safe, quiet place to live, having access to mental health and spiritual resources, access to clean foods and clean water and having a community of friends and reliable others to call upon or having the capacity to go rent a car and drive upstate to see the foliage . . . all those things were made possible because there have been pathways made clear for me, and people that I know, to bring my genius and creativity and innovation into spaces. I don't have to work hard past my trauma in order to work my way up the ladder; I can just bring it all of me, as I am into the space and do what it is that God has called me to do.

Ify: When you are saying this, I'm actually thinking that organizationally, true leadership that is invested in equity in our lifetime would then need to support beyond the worker's life cycle. For people to really be in concert with our humanity, they would have to see labor, which is a trade of our time for a benefit of the resources that we need to try to get ahead, they would be in concert with the "*ahead*" already—the future. They would say,

"It's actually not just about if this person leaves here, or even stays here for 10 to 15 years; it's about the ways that we use our resources to ensure that people have these pathways."

And I like that you're actually calling for the equity mindset within organizations to not only apply these truths—which they have to accept as truths first—about care and care models, that may be competing with the company's bottom line, but to push people to think　.

beyond just the physical or virtual space and more about the fact that human beings who are cycling in and out of these spaces, organizations benefit from them. So they need to be invested in as well. And the investment needs to be made into the full life of that human being, not just the life that human has while with the organization or while "on the job."

Alisha: It's a mindset of helping people reclaim their narrative. I think particularly white folks carry so much shame about their own shit that they don't know how to reclaim their narrative because their reclamation is to step on the heads and backs of other people, instead of recognizing that there's actually beauty in your pain, beauty in your trauma if you are willing to reclaim it, in the spirit of Sankofa and I know many of them don't understand that.

Ify: Yes, in the spirit of Sankofa! It is so difficult to translate what it means to be progressive and moving forward while perpetually always looking back. But, to your point, there is something about not looking back, as a decision maker, which makes it disingenuous as to how you can actually relate to somebody who has inherited all the tropes.

Alisha: Yes! So, when you asked me about what mindset shifts are needed, there is so much work for them to do, but maybe there's a teaching moment, right? Asking them, have they ever had a conversation with a loved one, a spouse, a parent and you are talking to them, but they are ignoring you? How did that make you feel? Then for them to connect that feeling to the very human feeling that certain people have always felt, due to systems in place. And even though this small example does not compare to hundreds of years that Black people have experienced, I feel like this may be the only way to get

white people to understand the mindset shift that
needs to occur.

Ify: This reminds me of the movie *A Time to Kill* and Matthew
McConaughey has the jury close their eyes and with this
amazing southern essence he takes them through the
predatory nature of the stalking of a young girl, the rape,
the torture, and attempted murder . . . and then he asks
them to imagine she's white. He then says, "The defense
rests, Your Honor." It's the way he uniquely brought the
story, that is a human story, and had them sit with what
was uncomfortable.

What my book explores is how you reconcile your
own identity as the starting point of being a
designer . . . because equity is about design. If you can't
actually answer the questions, "When was the first time
you knew that you were a particular race? When was the
first time you can remember feeling othered? When was
the first time you witnessed somebody feeling othered?
What were you, if anything, taught about intervening if
somebody else was bullied? If you can't answer those
questions then to your point, that is the work of a practitioner. I'm not saying everybody should do it, but the
work of the practitioner is that sometimes you're actually
going to have to bring folks to our narratives by placing
them in small pieces of what we endure every day. I
know some people think it's not our work; I definitely
don't think it is the work we all should be doing. But to
your point, it is a possible teaching moment for those
with that gift.

Finally, I think we have a way to go toward empathy,
even within our own community of how we view single
mothers, which I think even by name is problematic,
because most single mothers, unless they locked

themselves in a closet, are not "single mothers." They are in communities, they are in cultures, they are in spaces that intentionally create thriving, and even in two–parent households, many families are still matriarchal. There is a strength in the nurturing of womanhood and matriarchal–led spaces. And we have that in abundance, as a People.

But I do think that to create the radicalness that your organization is trying to innovate is the reclamation of that abundance. The abundance that society gets from us, we are creating conditions to also benefit from it so we can live our full lives. Y'all have been living your full lives off of Black mothers, who have been the original forced community of wet nurses, as well as forced psychologists and healers. I think that when you are talking about reclamation, we also can't shy away from that grueling labor of what it has meant to build this society and then to be told that pain is your birthright, or worse yet, shame.

Lastly, you brought up location and how we cannot disconnect the regionality when we are discussing equity.

Alisha: Exactly. That location piece is the key because equity is equity, but it damn sure looks different in the South than in Oregon.

Ify: Period.

13

Pipelines Are Deep Work: What You Should Know and Be Prepared For

Designing pipelines is no joke. One of the first major projects I was tasked with leading as the executive deputy director of the New York City Mayor's Office was a three-year strategy to recruit 1,000 Black, Latino, and Asian men to become public school teachers. The announcement was made during the wave of the My Brother's Keeper Initiative, a campaign created by President Barack Obama's administration in response to the murder of Trayvon Martin and several other unarmed Black boys and men. It felt like every week, I was asked for program updates—and that made me anxious. At that time, 45 percent of all NYC students were boys of color, yet only 7 percent of all educators were men of color (which was higher than other cities, which ranged from 2 to 4 percent, nationally).

I'm honored that the program is not only still in existence, but is thriving as one of the leading teacher-diversity efforts in the nation. But designing this pipeline exposed me to the following observations:

- Many within institutions who claimed to desire more diverse candidates were not prepared for that representation, or what that meant for them personally or as an organization.
- Most organizations that desire more representation have not seriously asked why underrepresentation is a problem.
- There is often more enthusiasm about recruitment, but less attention to the experiences of underrepresented persons once they enter into a new culture. This opens the door to harm upon arrival and retention challenges.
- Training of current managers and leadership is not a priority unless it is part of the pipeline design.
- The expectations for especially candidates of color is much higher than for white candidates. This is important because it means default biases around "fit" and "preference" are embedded as early as the application and selection processes.
- Creative methods that are rooted in some form of cultural competence can be viewed as a threat by those without proximity to the culture of those they are seeking to recruit.

Key ways to build an effective pipeline strategy include:

1. **Research:** I invested a lot of time not only researching recruitment strategies, but sustainability strategies. Because I did not know what I did not know, I created an exhaustive list of questions I anticipated my team would need to design for. Here are some of the questions that emerged:

Teacher Preparation	• What is the journey to become a teacher?
	• How can someone who didn't major in education become a teacher?
	• What is the cost of teacher certification, and are there prep supports?
	• Are there non-traditional routes toward becoming a teacher?
	• What agencies handle teacher preparation?
Teacher Recruitment	• How does the city currently recruit people to teach?
	• What are the current messaging strategies, and who designs them?
	• What are the narratives that would compel one to transfer their skills into the field of education?
	• What schools are we recruiting from?
	• Who is the face of recruitment?
Teacher Data	• What are the attrition trends? Are they different based on ethnicity and race?
	• What are the rewards and challenges current educators of color face?
	• What does support look like for teachers in general? Are there differences for teachers of color?
	• What are the national trends, and how do they compare to the rest of the nation?
	• Do we know why teachers are leaving?

Attitudes about Teaching and Education from Men of Color	• Why is a male teacher of color strategy necessary? • For those currently teaching, what are your thoughts about what support looks like that are unique to your counterparts? • What are the socio-emotional and economic factors to be considered?
Structural Barriers	• What is it about the teacher pipeline that has resulted in men being disproportionately out of the classroom? • What parts of the teacher recruitment and hiring process do we need to consider, including the application process? • Have there been any equity concerns about the current testing process?
Budget and Personnel	• What teams do we need to work on this project? • Who are the leading experts we need to retain? • What is the budget? • Are we able to hire people who sit in each of the agencies that touch the teacher recruitment, preparation and support departments?

As you can see, the research questions include identifying barriers, creating space to learn about attitudes about the profession, and understanding effective messaging strategies.

2. **Design a Trusted Team:** Effective pipelines require team members from different disciplines and functions. Being organized about who holds core functions, like research, operations, and data tracking, ensures that the equity strategy moves through more efficiently and with fewer hurdles. Also recognize that pipeline strategies also breed micro and macro

aggressions—especially when you are trying to increase the presence of Black and Brown bodies into very white spaces. Having a team is a way for everyone to get the support they need.

3. **Prioritize Wellness and Psychological Safety for Potential Candidates:** There were key features we embedded within the program. For example, schools who participated in our recruitment strategy were encouraged to hire at least two candidates, which would at least ensure that none of the new hires were there by themselves and had a professional partner experiencing the same process. We also identified partners who wanted to support the socio-emotional well-being of male teachers of color—from mental health to professional peer spaces. Even if your space can't provide all the perks, partnerships support filling in the gaps.

4. **Create Informal Leadership Opportunities:** Every organization can't promise a promotion, but they can invest in how candidates showcase their talents. Every year there's an NYC Men Teach showcase, where teachers get to demonstrate their unique styles of teaching, often embedding cultural twists to traditional pedagogical methods. This opportunity provides a platform to expand how professionalism is rewarded and acknowledged within the teaching profession.

5. **Advocate for a Team to Keep the Work Going:** The success of the work today is purely because of the investment of those hired to do this work. It was important that our design created opportunities to hire people outside of the organization. This freshness created a precedent for honesty, transparency, and accountability. The people who do the work are just as important as the people on the other side of the pipeline.

Remembering Our Radical Past While Demanding a Radical Now

By Anthony Smith (he/him), CEO of Cities United

We have to have conversations with each other and figure out what we are willing to fight for. I don't think we've ever done that before. I was on the phone with some people yesterday, and one of them said that what we're doing now is going to be the change for the next generation. But I want to see it today. If we keep saying to ourselves that we won't see change for generations, then we won't. So how do we shift the conversation to say, "We can actually make change today"? This idea that it took us generations to get here, so it's gonna take a generation to get out of here is a false narrative.

And even when we fight, can we sustain it? With every act of violence against a Black body, people went to the streets. But then things died down, and we went right back to where we were before the event. There are things that have changed, but have we changed as a collective?

Blacks used to be, as a collective, in thriving spaces that we built. We had the Black Wall Street, the Harlems, thriving neighborhoods. How do we get back to some of that, where imagination was happening? Where upward mobility was? Where equity was? If community is what we want, why do we have flight to the suburbs? Why don't we move back to these neighborhoods with these abandoned houses and thrive?

I think part of our job in this work is to call these things out and hold our own selves accountable. And we have to be honest about where there are still divisions within our community. I think in our community, we actually give preference and create more opportunities for Black men than we do for Black women. And even Black women do that right? Even when I'm talking to the women they always want to say what the men need. There have been plenty of Black men and Black fathers movements. We know we build better when our counterparts are also whole. That is just one of many examples of where equity mindset shifts are needed, internally.

To achieve equality, we must master equity. Equity is a precursor to equality because it centers the truth of harm, the realities of generational oppression, and the impact that has had on how populations are able to exist as full human beings. To skip this work is not only a sign of privilege, it is also the most common symptom of white-dominant culture and supremacy. Doing equity work is doing humanity work.

And it is a choice.

14

Reimagining "Chief": Ways Leaders Are Designing with an Equity Mindset

The term "chief" is often used in the business world to indicate seniority, expertise, and authority. In addition to its cousins "president," "partner," and "executive director," the prefix "chief" describes the highest-ranking officer within a division or department. We know that a chief executive officer (CEO) is the highest-ranking officer in a company and is responsible for making major decisions; a chief financial officer (CFO) is responsible for managing the financial aspects of a company; a chief operating officer (COO) is responsible for overseeing the day-to-day operations of a company; and so on. As a group, they are called "the C-suite," with the assumption that one with a chief-type role has power and influence within the organization and between each other. It is also assumed that they are responsible for the overall health of the organizational culture, including its commitment to equity, diversity, and inclusion.

In practice, however, all "chiefs" aren't created equally. The majority of Fortune 500 organizations, as well as leading nonprofits, have some form of diversity and inclusion mission statement, yet there is a reality about the composition of senior leaders across industries: they are overwhelmingly white, male, and older. A study highlighted that for companies whose gross revenue was greater than $500 million, 60 percent of the senior leadership team was white; 56 percent were male.[1] While diversity may increase within non-leadership roles, managerial and senior leadership roles remain mostly white, and often are the hardest spaces to diversify. The steady trend has been made to increase diversity through various efforts promoting increased awareness to racial underrepresentation, such as partnerships with historically Black colleges and universities, commonly referred to as HBCUs, and Hispanic-serving institutions, or HSIs; and statements and pledges to support movements on the ground, especially after the 2020 murders of George Floyd and Breonna Taylor by law enforcement. The coronavirus pandemic also provided an opportunity for collective attention to social and health disparities disproportionately experienced by communities of color and persons with disabilities. As a result, more business leaders were announcing wellness support for employees. It is worth noting that these responses to real equity concerns not only shifted the labor experiences of millions of people, but these moves also helped the image and branding of businesses. Keep that tucked away for a second.

Within two and half years from the global uprisings demanding justice in response to Black death and systemic racism, there were some indications that business leaders were starting to drift away from progressive efforts connected to more representation and inclusion of underrepresented communities. Funding to innovators of color, especially Black founders—which was already marginal compared to funding to white counterparts—has declined. Business predictions around recessions have led to mass layoffs, disproportionately impacting Black and Brown workers. Chief diversity officers are being laid off at a higher rate than other C-suite roles, and the majority of those losing their jobs are Black and women. Furthermore, discussions around long-standing workforce issues are more mainstream, including misogynoir—the unique discrimination Black women face, mental health stressors from bosses trying to go back to "business as usual," including demanding people to come back to their cubicles, and continued disparities in power and decision making. But there's another interesting dynamic: the rising pool of job seekers are likely the most socially conscious ever, with expectations ranging from hybrid work options to expressed commitments to social issues from those in leadership. This presents a great environment for problem solving and real equity beyond the standard diversity and inclusion package. Part of this includes redefining what it means to be a "chief" on a mass level. For guidance, I look to a space not often thought of as a model in the workspace: African villages.

In my parents' culture, the head chief or traditional ruler is referred to as "Eze." My late uncle, Chima, was an Eze. Of the many hats he wore, he was seen as an administrator of justice, a conflict resolutionist and a custodian of traditions. What intrigued me the most about his role was that it also symbolizes unity, holding the responsibility of bringing together members of the community, promoting harmony and cooperation among them, advocating for the needs and interests of his community, and building relationships with other groups and villages. The more I learned about this role, the more I recognized that there are models of leadership where being in power does not necessarily equate operating hierarchically. And that "order" is less about control, and more about maintaining peace, collaboration, and inclusion. I also understood that even in transactional operations— like trade or community agreements with other tribes—there are still communal considerations at play. The better my Uncle Chima performed these duties, the stronger the community was, both internally and to the public.

My title within my company—chief equity weaver—may appear to be a clever spin on the traditional corporate power role, but it was actually informed by my connection to my culture and my intention to support leaders who are attempting to find practical, measurable ways to bridge the gap between what is, and what we deserve. My goal when I started designing our Equity, Leadership and Culture™ platform was to focus less on the outcomes of diversity and inclusion, and more on supporting leaders with the most privilege, power, and access to understand the process of equity, and how to embed it in every aspect of their workplace. The theory is that the more leaders who are committed to seeing equity as part of their work, not a separate goal, the more sustainable outcomes for the entire culture. And as members of the community, that also means that leaders need safe spaces to ideate, experiment, share truths, and be encouraged when things get rough or when they fall short. And as a facilitator, I, too, get to engage fully in co-designing spaces that aim to be safer and fairer for those present, and those to come.

While the needs of each client vary from the next, I'm humbled that one of my clients, Lori Fresina, executive director of Voices for Healthy Kids—a project with the American Heart Association—granted me permission to highlight some of the work we've engaged in over three years to demonstrate how leaders can use their role to strengthen the organization's culture. I also want to shout out April Wallace from that team, who now formally leads their equity work and was part of the reason I ended up supporting her team. Black women stay finding ways to shift the culture—whether we have the title or not.

Leaders with an Equity Mindset Model Commitment and Vulnerability

Lori was present and engaged at every in-person and virtual team workshop and training. As a result, all of the managers who reported to her were present. Her presence was one of a learner, but in the moments when needs were shared by team members, she stepped into a role of advocate and designer, trying to figure out how to embed those needs that deepened equity into existing strategic plans and budgets. Lori was also open to being more transparent with her team about internal and external barriers, power dynamics, and politics which could impact how swiftly the team moved. This goes to one of the characteristics of an equity mindset (EM): advancing equity is about being strategic. Transparency invites a broader community of problem solvers to respond to institutional standards that are too big for one person to address. Leaders who model more participatory processes also build greater trust with team members and support how each member—including the Chief—holds themselves accountable to the larger group.

Some of the ways commitment to equity was demonstrated included:

- Regularly scheduled sessions, trainings, and workshops as part of regular professional development;
- Creating equity missions, visions, and practices for the organization as a whole, as well as for each department—each reviewed annually;
- Investing in coaching for each of the senior leaders, including herself.

Leaders with an EM Identify How White-Dominant Culture Impacts Their Organization and Then Practice Different Behaviors

Confession: it is not always easy (for me) to talk to cultures about whiteness. But the reality is that we all operate under a white-dominant framework, and many of our institutions are microcosms of the status quo. Openness to discussions around learned behavior, mapping how it shows up in the work, and getting support on alternative ways of being support how each member learns how to spot harmful dominant behaviors that were once unquestioned or undetectable. Here are some of the ways team members chose different behaviors and practices:

	Dominant Normal Practice	Applying an Equity Mindset
Communications' Vendors	Contracting the same long-standing white-led communications firm, even for content related to equity	Contracting a person of color-led firm with experience in communication about the organization in a culturally competent manner
Using BIPOC[2] as a catchall	Lumping all communities of color under the "BIPOC" umbrella, with almost no distinction as to the different marginalized experiences between each community	Writing the full names of each community, highlighting their unique experiences where applicable
Turnaround of Work Product	Frustration over missed deadlines that pushed back meeting internal deadlines	More time to learn each person's work style and creating more space for activities often unaccounted for while working, like processing, drafting, and researching

	Dominant Normal Practice	Applying an Equity Mindset
Advisory Committees	Mostly white academics and researchers grandfathered in, based on existing relationships within the organizations	Researchers with both lived and academic experiences, with more specific expertise on the impact of disparities on marginalized communities
Identifying Priority Policy Areas	Internally created by the organization, which informs their legislative work, as well as the grants they make available to the public	Engaged with leaders and members of impacted communities to inform the organization on the issues that mattered to them—as well as ensured community groups within priority communities received support to apply for grants

Leaders with an EM Support Experimentation

There were two major movements I was proud to support the Voices team with. The first was in supporting the creation of the new senior equity manager role, with April as the inaugural leader. The second was in quickly advocating that one person cannot be responsible for all of the equity and culture work. From my experience, it is unsustainable for one person to hold all of the equity work, and usually the expectations from the organization are too high and connected to broader ROI (return on equity) goals of the organization, rather than as an extension of equity commitments. One person building an entire equity focus also doesn't create a culture of shared responsibility.

April and I began designing a rotational equity and culture cohort, a professional development opportunity that engages some of the team members for six months at a time, with each member exploring ways to implement more equitable practices within one area of the internal or external work. One person is designing an internal accountability metric to ensure smaller businesses of color are being engaged during the vendor process. Another cohort member is exploring ways the organization could support the vertical trajectory of those not interested in being in management. Another is researching how to embed equity as an organizational operations priority. The topics are super dope and relevant. The goal is not for each person to be an expert, but rather for everyone to participate in defining the culture they want to work in. At the conclusion of the cohort, the team presents recommended practices to be adopted into the team's equity and culture guide. Then a fresh new group will engage in the next cohort, building upon what the last group had started. Lori approved the strategy, in addition to supporting a summit that provides space for team building, visioning, and individual coaching. At this organization, equity is a community priority, one that is building a new professional norm around experimentation to find solutions.

Creating Space for Partners to Engage in Equity Design and Problem Solving

When Lori asked me to come speak with the Strategy Advisory Committee (SAC) about power mapping, I was excited. Training some of the leading non-profit leaders in the country on movement strategies was important to me because almost all of them led policy work that touched communities I was connected to. Similar to the role my uncle once held, engaging with leaders outside of her immediate organization signaled to partners not only that this was the work Voices was committed to doing, but also that Voices is a willing collaborator in how they advance their equity work.

And maybe that's where I'll end this piece: with the hope that more leaders see how equity is a tool to create the spaces so many of us deserve to be in—and perhaps lead in. It just requires a different orientation and a commitment to continually surround ourselves with more tools, resources, and, most importantly, a village.

Don't Talk About It: Be About It

By Dr. David J. Johns (he/him), Executive Director National Black Justice Coalition

In this moment, what comes to mind is the importance of people in positions of leadership who purport to care about or value equity. And by that I mean, at a minimum, how such leaders meaningfully include our people. Anyone in that position by choice or appointment—who also claims to care about equity—should appreciate that almost everyone's life outcomes and opportunities in the United State, as well as countries that have been colonized by white nationalists' supremacist ideology, are saturated with what Black feminists refer to as "the measures of domination," which are the signs, systems, and symbols that allow white supremacy and patriarchy, and homophobia and transphobia, misogynoir, and ableism to remain, with no real indication of being discarded. Being aware of that fact and how one operates as a leader in the system that they are responsible for is required for someone who cares about designing and holding "just" spaces and doing any work anchored in equity.

Related to that, at this moment, it's important for me to name that a part of what should be appreciated in these spaces

(Continued)

is that not everyone's voices, values, or perspectives should be centered. I look forward to more leaders asking the question and then testing it out, but then also sitting back. Especially those with ultimate power, access, and privilege.

How different would conversations around justice and equity be if white people or people in positions of privilege just did the work in silence?

#EquityMindset with Ross Moskowitz

Ross Moskowitz (he/him) is an attorney and ally

Ify: I don't know if white people really listened to other white people around their equity journeys.

Ross: That's interesting because I've never heard it framed that way: *Do white people listen to other white people?* I have never really thought about that, but it's a good question.

Ify: Part of the reason why I asked that question is because however you slice it, the majority of our for-profit and nonprofit government spaces are still predominantly white led, white male led, with some organizations doing better than others on an individual basis. And even in the DEI space, studies show that the majority of people in those spaces are also white. So, I am curious to know what are some of the things that we may need to learn or "unlearn" regarding equity in a broad sense. Especially in for-profit capitalist spaces. All of us have inherited a

capitalist mindset, and one of my theories is that capitalism and equity compete with each other.

Ross: Sure, they're not necessarily aligned. I totally agree with
you. There's this pie, and it can only be split up in so
many ways. So how do you get in on that? Because
giving opportunity is one thing and letting someone have
a seat at the table. But if they then don't have an ownership piece of that table, how far can they really go?

I come from a privileged background but not at a level
that allowed me to just never worry. So going to my law
firm was never in the cards for me. So, tripling my salary
when I was a third-year associate, all of a sudden, allowed
me to start saving money and buy an apartment. So
there's your first equity play, right? So equity begets
equity, right? Then when we got a bigger family and
decided to move, I had equity now in an asset that I
could sell that allowed me to buy a bigger place. So once
you're in that, it's no different than just a real estate play.
You start buying property and if the property appreciates
a little bit, you refinance it and start to build your portfo-
lio. You start building up your equity; it gives you that
freedom, that ownership.

So going back to where this conversation started,
to me, getting a seat at the table, to your comment about
"unlearn," there are still folks who think a seat at the
table is enough. And, yeah, that's a criticism; I'm trying
not to make it a judgment, but there are people who
think, *Well, Ify is at the table, what else does she need?* And
not always thinking about their journey, and what their
journey has afforded them.

Ify: Or what else do they need, if we're being honest, right? Because they're looking at me as everything I am supposed to represent.

Ross: Right. So, if you're at the table, but you're not either developing the equity or building clients or given the opportunity to build your book of business, or you know, in a corporate for-profit organization, we're going to promote Ify and we'll give her some shares too. Because think about it, from a business sense, aren't you going to feel better and feel more incentivized to grow and to learn at your company if now you literally have shares at the company? So the success of the company can now translate into dollars for you. If you look at some of the VCs, especially the minority-owned VCs, that's a lot of what occurs, right? A raising of angel money to throw back into the cohort for the next person's project. Pay it forward.

So the seat at the table, from my perspective of unlearning, is not enough. Also, this idea of allyship is something I continue to struggle with. Not in a bad way, it's just a challenge, and I feel like I still have to kind of check myself, right? For example, Ify is in a meeting with six or seven other people and the senior white guy makes a comment that isn't a "shark bite," but it's like a little mosquito bite. It's clear the comment is bothering you. After the meeting, I go over to you and say, "I'm really sorry Bob made that comment. I think that was inappropriate." And you're like, "Okay." Well, I gotta unlearn that, because what I really have to do is right then and there in that setting, in a way that doesn't embarrass Bob, say, "Hey, Bob, that's not right, man. You need to check that statement." Again, it has to be done in a way that Bob hears it. So that's something else I need to unlearn. I thought pulling you aside after was the right thing, and maybe it was a few years ago, five years ago. But now, we're in an advanced space. I need to step in there. If I just come to you and not model what should be done, whatever effect I could have had, is gone.

Ify: I love this, and I love talking about this with another attorney because we can play a bit with the legal theory, if you will, of "critical mass." I love the concept of critical mass because it moves beyond the seat at the table, which is really about representation and for many folks that's where the conversation stays. But it also doesn't necessarily talk or fully flesh out what it means at times to be the only or to be the few; what it means to be at the table, but not empowered, right? Or not necessarily having assurances that you are able to fully "be," not even with different ideas, but even sometimes with your genius, right? The whole concept of critical mass was that it's not necessarily that just because there's another Black woman in the room, Ify is comfortable. But it is about how do we at least acknowledge that there is somewhat of a privilege of not having to think about who's in the room? And also acknowledge that being at the table presents challenges that are around cultural connection: being able to be seen and heard. I think that is why allyship is such a huge area because it is about the practice of seeing and hearing others, and being responsive to others. So, even as you're talking, referring to your meeting example, about going to Ify after the meeting may not be enough, I feel that it should be both the private approach, as well as, the public calling out of the harmful statement. Allyship is also about providing safety.

Ross: You're right, and I probably do that as well in those situations. You know, you said something that really resonated with me. The way I approach this is with my life experience, which I know is a different experience than yours, for instance. But having said that, we all have degrees of impostor syndrome, right? I don't care how confident you are, I don't care if there's six white male Jews in the room and we're all the same age and we all make the same money. Let's just declare that everyone's at the table equally and we all own the same amount of the company. We all got there differently, so everyone has a degree of imposter syndrome. So, to your point, if I have a degree of imposter syndrome, but I see six other male Jewish faces around the table and we own equally, my reaction is night and day if now we add an African American woman and she sits in there and looks around and says, "Huh, okay where's my critical mass?"

So, critical mass is a seat at the table, but it's way more than that. Do you literally have a decision and an outcome? Is your voice not just a voice that's there for the record, right? Or is your voice actually helping to shape a conversation and a recognition of your experience? I mean, the basic element of D&I, in my view, is that having your view, my view, and other diverse views can only make us better. It doesn't mean we land on your view, it doesn't mean we land on my view, but it's just a better way of thinking to have all different experiences at the table. The more, the merrier, so to speak. But, it has to be real, it has to be genuine. It can't be the idea that okay, we hired Ify and she has a seat at the table, but it's really us six Jewish men running the company.

Ify: Practically speaking, it's hard, and again, this entire inquiry and these conversations are to amplify what is complex about this, right? But, practically speaking, even if there are four or five Black people and people of color in the room and an equal number of five white men and women—you're right, there's this goal of people who have diverse ways of looking at things. But I also think that we don't level-set on the differences as it relates to power. I don't think that we talk enough about *that* difference in the room. We don't talk enough about the fact that when I come into that space there isn't a kind of grounding of "Welcome, Ify, as you may have noticed there are five white people here and we are doing our best in these areas, but we also can't say that you are not going to at times experience the following side effects of being in this space."

Ross: Welcoming someone into space, I couldn't agree with you more. Letting them know that we're going to make this as smooth as we can, but there are going to be bumps. But, let me flip that, where we are in the same meeting example and ample warning has been given, a comment is made and you don't like it. And you say, "Hey, Ross, you know, I'm not happy with that comment. I don't know what you intended by that." And I say, "Ify, I didn't intend anything. I never intended to harm." You can apologize all you want and say that the intention wasn't there, but it still happened. So, where's the line? In other words, with the introduction or welcoming statement you made a moment ago, this almost gives people a pass to act or continue to act poorly—i.e. "Ify, I told you that this might happen."

Ify: Right, I agree. But I do want to say this, I think the last
part around critical mass that business spaces don't recognize is that allyship is great and should not go away. We've
gone deeper into how it can look in different ways,
including sponsorship and how there are different levels of
investment and allyship.

I also think that part of what gets missed is that in that
same meeting, for example, when that person says, "I
didn't intend it that way," when there are more people
that may have been culturally proximate to that type of
microaggression in their own lives, then the issue doesn't
have to be "me and that person" conversation. We
embrace the likelihood that other people who can relate
adds another value to the organization so that it's not just
Ify holding it, or even her ally holding it. It then becomes
a learning opportunity and can become a discussion point.

Ross: I love that phrase you said, "holding it." That phrase
resonates with me, and I can immediately identify how
important it is to have the critical mass, right? Everyone
sort of has all these stories about people who have paved
the way for others, but a lot of them do it on their own.
So think about that. That they had to do it on their own.
So that's another level that I don't think people always
appreciate: people who have succeeded in white-
dominated society, that, on their own. They held, to your
point, they held that stuff all the way through. They may
have had allies, but they held that. So that's a really, really
good way of thinking about it. Also, going back and
coming full circle, if there's a critical mass in the room,
not only do you get to share that hold, but one would

hope the unlearning could happen sooner. Because now the comments made are heard by multiple people, and so maybe there's a moment of pause on the part of the speaker to read the room and reassess the audience.

If you choose to commit to an equity mindset, you will struggle. Frederick Douglass warned us that we can't have transformation without a struggle. *"If there is no struggle there is no progress. Those who profess to favor freedom and yet deprecate agitation are men who want crops without plowing up the ground; they want rain without thunder and lightning. They want the ocean without the awful roar of its many waters."* If we're in this, we're in this.

We are disciples of struggle in pursuit of progress.

Epilogue

Act I: Oh, I'm Messy, Too

I grew up an Eagles fan and an overall football fan: faithfully looking forward to hearing the matchup when my family came back home from church on Sundays, and getting all riled up Monday nights when the theme song would come on. But like many others, the brutality of the game that disproportionately impacted Black bodies, the lopsidedness of white team ownership, and the problematic handling of Colin Kaepernick's stance on police brutality and racial injustice resulted in me making a personal decision to divest from the game. And it wasn't easy—especially when the Eagles won the Super Bowl in 2018. I remember refreshing my Twitter feed after the game was over, just to catch the comments and the brashness of a community that I grew up loving. Disconnecting from spaces you love is difficult, even when you know they're problematic.

Confession: I briefly broke my boycott of the NFL during the 2023 matchup between the Philadelphia Eagles and the Kansas City Chiefs. Actually (confession number two) I broke it two weeks prior to watch the Eagles win the NFC championship (which I also missed in 2018) but also to watch the Kansas City Chiefs lose to the Cincinnati Bengals. In my mind, it mattered that the Chiefs lost for one reason and one reason only: their name. As their name—as well as chants and fan traditions—still possess tropes, stereotypes, and the violent narratives associated with Native American communities, I wanted them to lose. Even if their head coach was a beloved Eagles coaching alum (sorry, Andy). But in a squeaker, Kansas won. And I was frustrated. Because me watching the Super Bowl meant I was going to see all the problematic rituals all over again.

Super Bowl LVII was exactly what you'd expect: a production. I was there for the Eagles because I felt like I couldn't miss another championship victory (they lost). And I was also there for Rihanna because . . . Rihanna. And when I saw the Eagles run out of the jumbotron onto the field, I felt like that loyal fan all over again. My sister screamed, doing the latest TikTok dances as she celebrated their entrance. The memories of Eagles of the past, from quarterbacks Randall Cunningham and Donovan McNabb, to the now and future in Jalen Hurts had me proud to support a team that had a deep history of "us" with the ball and in leadership positions that were historically seen as too sophisticated for Black athletes. Yes, I was conflicted enjoying the opening this much. I'm human and can admit it was a good feeling.

My mood started to shift as the traditional anthems began. I expected them. What I didn't expect was the mixed feelings I felt around Danny Collins, a deaf Navajo Native American sign language interpreter, performing "America the Beautiful" in a crowd of fans who still do the tomahawk chop. I just kept saying out loud, "I wonder what he is thinking." I thought about the honor and dignity he represented for so many people: Native Americans, deaf people, disabled people. I also thought about the dishonor of this nation and didn't know how to take the performance. I still don't know what to say except that it matters to me that he felt it was an honor.

I couldn't help, however, but to go down the rabbit hole of seeing if there were any thoughts from other Indigenous folks around the Super Bowl. I came across a series of quotes in an article that helped me connect with my internal conflict:

I'm just really grateful that they did highlight our people because I think it's really important. [As for the] "tomahawk chop" I think that's the only thing that really bothers me about that whole thing is that, and I don't know where it came from. And I don't really fully understand it, but it is almost like a mockery.

—a Native American hoop dancer and member of the Hopi-Tewa and Choctaw nations who performed at the Super Bowl

I think we should keep it. I mean we need to be respectful about it. I understand but I mean it's a tradition.

—a University of Kansas psychology major, described as hollering as she did "the open-handed chop with the crowd"

If they don't think it is okay to do then maybe we should stop. But the Native Americans I've come in contact with have said that they didn't have any issues with it. Basically it is all opinion-based. We've gone a long way to make sure that we are respectful of everybody's culture and being vigilant about it.

—a technician from Kansas City, Missouri, who also backed his case up by sharing all the changes the franchise had undergone, including the retirement of "Warpaint," the live mascot, a horse named "Warpaint" once ridden by a man with a headdress on[1]

There's so much to unpack here, which I invite you to help me do. I want to first start with where I began: in the mirror. As someone who has been on the ground globally, observing injustices, organizing with fellow movement leaders, and advocating for more just legislation, I also have moments when I operate with contradictions and hypocrisies. One could chalk it up to me just being human, and this is a good time for me to pause and remind myself that I am allowed and deserving of the full breadth of what humanity affords—even ignorance and cognitive dissonance. One would also not be wrong in raising the burden it takes to always be conscious; virtually everything we're connected to in our culture stems from the same painful origin of Native American genocide, enslavement of people of African descent—followed by Jim Crow, Jane Crow, and ongoing policy evolutions of slave and Black codes, and the exploitation of the poor, the immigrant, and the disabled. But as a practitioner, there's something about being in these moments and remembering agreements and commitments you made to yourself—especially those that stem from an awareness and acknowledgment of the entangled relationship between communities' survival and the systems that stifle their full humanity.

Before I unpack, I want to throw one more perspective into the mix, which comes from Rhonda LeValdo, a Haskell Indian Nations University professor, Acoma Pueblo activist, and founder of the Not In Our Honor coalition:

> Our people were rounded up, kids stolen from their families, sent to boarding schools . . . and stripped of their culture and identity. Their religion was outlawed, they could not practice their ceremonies, they couldn't sing their songs. So why is it OK for the fans in Kansas City to play Indian, when our people weren't allowed to be Indian?[2]

If that shit doesn't hit you, then I'm not sure what will.

I'm thinking about the ways Rhonda's statement connects to Danny Collins of the Navajo tribe, skilled in both American and Native sign language, who's labor modeled inclusion, connecting deaf audiences to the game—even though his interpretation was of a song that asks for God to bless the colonizers on the land once protected by the interpreter's ancestors.

I'm thinking about how one stadium can hold the sentiments of the hoop dancer, working while representing their Hopi-Tewa and Choctaw communities, and attendees who believe that (white) traditions trump the continued subjugation of Native Americans—and minimizing the offense as "opinions-based."

I'm thinking about the times I have been in spaces where my truth was minimized while working. And where the enjoyment others assumed of my culture—even the harmful stereotypes—was deemed as much more of a priority than my dignity.

And I also can say that I have compromised my stances occasionally to enjoy what I wanted to. And I have caused harm more times than I can count, regardless of whether I had the power to impact another's well-being.

This is not a statement to make all offenses equal; I definitely do not believe that to be the case. This is just a transparent moment for me to share the ways our culture makes it hard for even marginalized communities to disrupt systems; how hard it is to find joy that isn't tainted with racialized capitalism or the necessary ignorance needed to just relax and unwind. I am wrapped in it, too—and working on myself every day.

Act II: The Language of Becoming What We Want

This work continues to expand my perspective of what's possible. As an attorney, I know how important words are to our very existence as a people. But a conversation with my sister-girl, friend, and founder of (Un)Learning Space, Lydia Mercer, challenged me with how we paint the future using our language in a more vivid, explicit way. She simply said:

> The language that we use, thinking about it, and how powerful it is, like, anti-racism, anti-oppression, all of the language that we're using talks about what we can't do and who we're not. So I'm moving to a place where we are talking and reimagining and speaking what we want to be, in the affirmative, and what we want to be true. And I know that we don't know exactly what that fully looks like, but that's the beautiful space that I want to be in.

That's the beautiful space I want to be in, too. Onward.

Notes

Chapter 4

1. https://theantioppressionnetwork.com/resources/saferspacepolicy/.

Chapter 6

1. Kerry Patterson, Joseph Grenny, Ron McMillan, Al Switzler, and Emily Gregory, *Crucial Conversations: Tools for Talking When the Stakes Are Too High* (McGraw-Hill Education eBooks, 2013).

Chapter 7

1. According to findings from The Global Workplace Analytics and Owl Labs, at the height of the pandemic, 70 percent of full-time workers switched to remote working completely. Ninety percent of those surveyed said their productivity levels were the same or higher at home. **One in three people reported they would quit their jobs if they were no longer allowed to work remotely after the pandemic.** https://owllabs.com/state-of-remote-work/2021.

2. See the American Bar Association's article, "Will Working from Home Be a Reasonable Accommodation Post-COVID?" https://www.americanbar.org/groups/gpsolo/publications/gpsolo_ereport/

2020/november-2020/will-working-home-be-reasonable-accom modation-post-covid/.

Chapter 8

1. https://www.catalyst.org/reports/antiracism-workplace-leader ship/.
2. Colorism is the prejudice or discrimination against individuals with a dark skin tone, typically among people of the same ethnic or racial group. Texturism is the idea that certain textures of hair are indicators of a superior status in society. Loosely coiled hair, long hair, or hair that fits the standards associated with European features are accepted as societal norms; hair that is tightly coiled is often seen as a range of negative perceptions, including unkempt, unprofessional, and sometimes an assumption of class and education. Cissexism is the belief or assumption that cis people's gender identities, expressions, and embodiments are more natural and legitimate than those of trans people. Heterosexism is defined as the marginalization and/or oppression of people who are lesbian, gay, bisexual, queer, and/or asexual, based on the belief that heterosexuality is the norm.

Chapter 9

1. See Claudia Goldin, "Female Labor Force Participation: The Origin of Black and White Differences, 1870 and 1880," *Journal of Economic History* 37, no. 1 (1977): 87–108. https://dash.harvard .edu/handle/1/2643657.
2. Jacqueline Jones, *Labor of Love, Labor of Sorrow: Black Women, Work, and the Family from Slavery to the Present* (New York: Basic Books, 1985).
3. Deborah Gray White, "Making a Way Out of No Way," in *Too Heavy a Load: Black Women in Defense of Themselves, 1894–1994* (W.W. Norton & Company, 1999).

4. See National Partnership for Women & Families, 2022, "Black Women and the Wage Gap" Fact Sheet, https://nationalpartnership .org/wp-content/uploads/2023/02/african-american-women-wage-gap.pdf.

5. Center for American Progress, 2022, "Black Women Need Access to Paid Family and Medical Leave," https://www.americanpro gress.org/article/black-women-need-access-to-paid-family-and-medical-leave/.

6. Our team believes that the term "microaggressions" often minimizes the full harm experienced by those who receive such violence while trying to work. While this is the common term used for this occurrence, there is nothing "micro" about this constant experience.

7. McKinsey & Company, 2021, "Women in the Workplace 2021," https://www.mckinsey.com/featured-insights/diversity-and-inclusion/women-in-the-workplace.

8. National Women's Law Center, 2022, "Men Have Recouped Their Pandemic Related Labor Force Losses While Women Lag Behind," https://nwlc.org/wp-content/uploads/2022/02/January-Jobs-Day-updated.pdf.

Chapter 12

1. Monnica T. Williams, "Racism in Academic Publishing," *Psychology Today*, July 14, 2020, https://www.psychologytoday.com/us/blog/culturally-speaking/202007/racism-in-academic-publishing.

Chapter 14

1. See Weber Shandwick's 2019 report, "Paving the Way for Diversity & Inclusion Success," https://www.webershandwick.com/news/paving-the-way-for-diversity-inclusion-success/.

2. BIPOC stands for Black, Indigenous, and People of Color.

Epilogue

1. https://fox4kc.com/news/native-americans-grapple-with-chiefs-super-bowl-celebrations/.

2. https://www.kcur.org/news/2023-02-03/kansas-city-chiefs-racist-traditions-tomahawk-chop-native-american-violence-nfl-super-bowl-2023.

Acknowledgments

I want to start by thanking God, the spirit and original designer, sustainer, and strength-giver when I didn't have it.

To my dog, Bishop, who has been my confidante for a decade, protects his mom, and knows how to pick me up when things are a little tough.

To the family I was born into: the Ikes. Thank you all for the support, and special shout-out to my mother, Bernice, and my sister, God-Is Ike, for contributing to this book in big and small ways. To my dear friend Amber Cabral, the first one to encourage me to write this book, the pep-talker giver, the card sender just because, the one who gives, even with a demanding life. And the one who helped me cope with my new relationship with long COVID, reminding me that my body and mind are more than capable of finishing this work, even as I learn to work differently. Thanks, Friend.

To my chosen family and friends who rooted me on, checked up on my body, and reminded me that this book was already written—I just had to fill the pages. Some of you also lent your colorful insights and voices to this book—thank you: Agu Onuma, Alexis Confer, Alisha L. Gordon ,Anthony Smith, Christopher Dennis, David Johns, Dominique Morgan, Ember Phoenix, Ivelyse Andino, James R. Artis, Javier Lopez, Dr. Kelly Burton, L. Toni Lewis, MD, Linara Davidson

Greenidge, Lydia Mercer, Margaret G. Wilson, Michael Farber, Nana Gyamfi, Natalia Diaz, Nik Walker, Rebecca Cokley, Ross Moskowitz, Tyshaia Earnest, Whitney McGuire.

To my Pink Cornrows team: thank you all for helping me create more space for this work, for believing in me throughout this process, and for responding to the other parts of our work as I hunkered down to finish this project. You are a huge part of why *The Equity Mindset* even exists.

To the Wiley community, and a special shout-out to Jeanenne Ray. Being seen and heard by you through every stage of not only this process but the parts of my life that almost made me want to stop was crucial. Thank you for honoring when I needed breaks, rests, and extensions. It truly made a difference. And to Adaobi Obi Tulton, thank you for your editing support and affirmations, which gave me room to say what needed to be said—in the best way possible.

To my current and former clients who've trusted me with supporting your cultures with *The Equity Mindset* curriculum. It's been a pleasure to shift culture with you. So much of what I'm continuing to learn and build is because of the authenticity of the spaces we've co-created.

To the architects of legacy, our Ancestors, the majority of whom didn't have titles, or positions, or even the legal recognition of being human. Thank you for not letting any of that determine your humanity, for daring to escape, for yelling even when they called us dogs, for marching even when they called us rioters, for loving even when we had every reason to hate. I honor what you endured for me to be able to do this.

To my body still battling the impact of the pandemic. Thank you for being kind to me. Thank you for reconfiguring ways to remember things when thoughts were foggy and for telling me to rest when twitches made it hard for me to type. Thank you for holding me through a pandemic, for fighting COVID, for forgiving me when I kept you up too long, and for making three hours of sleep feel like eight. I have learned to love you more during this process.

And if you made it this far to the end of the acknowledgments, thank you. Because every being above is rooting for every being now and after us to have peace, dignity, and care. I hope you may experience that as well.

About the Author

Ifeomasinachi Ike (also called Ifeoma or Ify) is an award-winning artist, movement attorney, equity practitioner, researcher, and policy strategist. She is the founder of Pink Cornrows, a Black femme-led social impact agency that provides thought partnership, research, and equity-centered strategies across corporate, nonprofit, philanthropic and culture industries. Ify is also the founder of Black Policy Lab, an annual conference connecting practitioners, experts, and community to co-create policy solutions to address systemic inequity. Learn more at www.ifeomasinachi.com.

Index